# THE CODE OF CHRIST

�֍ ✖ ✖ ✖
✖ ✖
✖

# The
# CODE OF CHRIST

## An Interpretation
## of the Beatitudes

GERALD HEARD

*Wipf & Stock*
PUBLISHERS
*Eugene, Oregon*

Wipf and Stock Publishers
199 W 8th Ave, Suite 3
Eugene, OR 97401
www.wipfandstock.com

ISBN 13: 978-1-55635-173-0
ISBN 10: 1-55635-173-9

Publication date: 1/1/2008
Previously published by Harpers & Brothers, 1941

Photograph of Gerald Heard by Jay Michael Barrie

*To Three,*

# Series Foreword

Gerald Heard (Oct. 6, 1889–Aug. 14, 1971) wrote nearly forty books during the course of a distinguished career. His Cambridge-trained, curiosity-ridden mind left no stone unturned in its intellectual investigations. His nonfiction topics ranged from history to philosophy, from psychology to religion, and virtually everything in between. These issues were woven together by a single unifying theme—the evolution of consciousness. During the 1940s, after he had relocated to America, after he had rediscovered his religious roots, and after he had begun a rigorous daily meditation practice, Gerald, as he was always known, mobilized his energies into establishing Trabuco College in Southern California. Trabuco was the first coeducational spiritual community in America to incorporate ecumenical, nonsectarian religious principles and practices. And practice the Trabuco attendees did, meditating three times daily in order to accelerate the spiritual evolution of their own individual consciousnesses.

Having previously published a dozen mostly academic and popular science books, Gerald turned his attention to religion during this war-torn decade. Gerald's religious writings from this period consist of eight key contributions that address practical and inspirational spiritual themes. Of these, four primary Heardian reli-

i

gious works are initially included in this vital new Wipf & Stock series, with more to follow. Collectively these books comprise Gerald's quintessential statements on the spiritual path, and a person could conceivably use these volumes as guidebooks for their entire spiritual journey.

And here is Gerald at his very best—preaching the evolution of consciousness and offering practical advice on how to attain it. Gerald's rotating roles as visionary historian, maverick cosmologist, and prescient philosopher are all present in the background of these religious works. But at the forefront is Gerald the practicing mystic and knowing docent, gushing forth an ebullient but sometimes cautionary narrative on traversing the spiritual path from start to finish. His accounts, as confirmed by classic mystics and traditional texts, derive from his own subjective experience. The ringing truth of his musings will cause the receptive reader first to reflect, then to act, propelled by the stirring contagion of Gerald's boundless enthusiasm.

In the 1940s, novelist Christopher Isherwood wrote that Gerald, "has influenced the thought of our time, directly and indirectly, to an extent which will hardly be appreciated for another fifty years." Those fifty years have now passed. Some of Gerald's ideas have fallen by the wayside, while others lie dormant still waiting to sprout. Yet a good many have blossomed into unspoken cornerstones of contemporary thought. The widespread establishment of religious communities has become commonplace. Religious syncretism, ecumenical studies, and interdisciplinary, eclectic approaches lie at the vanguard of progressive religious thought. Contemplative meditation practices have gained broad acceptance across a spectrum of diverse traditions. Theories on the evolution of consciousness abound. Colleges and whole movements of thought now regularly explore the transpersonal realm of pure consciousness.

But what makes Gerald's farsighted approach to religion especially relevant now is what made it relevant when these books were first published—he is espousing timeless truths. The reader is supplied with a map, compass, and numerous exhortations of attainment, as well as warnings of the pitfalls to avoid while embarking on this singlemost important sojourn in life. Gerald offered no quick fixes or shortcuts. He advocated a wholesale restructuring of one's entire being through, "the skilled, conscious training of our spirits." He advanced a holistic approach long before holistic approaches became popular.

Within these books is found Gerald's essential message: "Our whole life must become intentional and purposive, instead of a series of irrelevant events, adventures, and accidents. We must ourselves deliberately develop ourselves. That evolution which follows will show itself in a threefold development: in growth of conduct, of character and of consciousness itself. The world exists for man to achieve union with God. The meaning of all, the purpose and the end of all is one thing, seeing God."

When revisiting Gerald's spiritual classics in this new century, we are entering the very heart of religious experience. We are treading the path trodden by serious spiritual practitioners, be they novices or seasoned mystics. We are undertaking a journey of utmost significance, leading to pulsating union with God. As able guide and modern interpreter of mysticism, Gerald Heard nimbly and authoritatively beckons us toward the Goal that each of us was born to realize in this very life.

John Roger Barrie
Literary Executor of Gerald Heard
Nevada City, California
January 22, 2007

Thanks especially to Ted Lewis of Wipf and Stock Publishers, and Craig Tenney and Phyllis Westberg of Harold Ober Associates for their valuable assistance in bringing this series into print.

For more information on Gerald Heard, visit geraldheard.com, the Gerald Heard Official Website.

—JRB

# CONTENTS

✠✠✠✠✠✠✠✠✠✠✠✠✠✠✠✠✠✠✠✠✠✠✠✠✠✠✠✠✠✠✠✠✠✠✠✠✠✠✠✠✠✠✠

# PREFACE

THE substance of these essays was given as seven addresses at the Mount Hollywood Congregational Church, Los Angeles, by the courtesy of the Minister, the Reverend Allan A. Hunter.

# INTRODUCTION

✦✦✦✦✦✦✦✦✦✦✦✦✦✦✦✦✦✦✦✦✦✦✦✦✦✦✦✦✦✦✦✦✦✦✦✦✦✦

The real obstacle to believing in Christianity is not miracle; no, not even such a miracle as a Virgin Birth and the Resurrection of a man killed by crucifixion. What really stands in the way of accepting the Gospel of Jesus is not the strain on our credulity but the demand on our characters. It is the Sermon on the Mount which is the central problem. First and foremost, it is not a question, "Can I believe that certain miraculous events happened to and were done by one man long ago?" But, rather, "Can I believe that certain moral miracles can happen to and be done by me?" If we could believe that the Sermon on the Mount was true, if it could work as a practical proposition in our present lives, then all the rest of the Gospel statements would certainly look far less improbable.

Such was the considered opinion of a scholarly modernist Episcopal minister. Its honesty is helpful. It brings out clearly two essential facts: Firstly, that Christianity is in essence, in "substance," a way of life for us to live. All the rest is "accident," accretions that illustrate or obscure, assist or obstruct our understanding and practicing the Way. Secondly, that this way of life when it is considered as such, and not as traditional poetry, strikes an honest mind as impossible as a miracle. We need this honesty because such honesty pays Christ the compliment of taking him seriously. It views carefully and narrowly his propositions, as critically as a good lawyer scans a proffered contract. Because of this scrutiny it cannot accept them, but at least it regards them as real proposals intended to apply to our actual situation. Until there is this frankness we can make no progress. At any cost we must get away from that other attitude, which treats Christ's gospel as poetry, "Pickwickian" poetry. "The world is out of joint," cry the tragic poets, the dark seers. "Very well," reply the religious romancers, "then just imagine that you have no joints: let imagination float you in a cloudy world of words upside down, as a duck floats when eating duckweed. Just put a negative against all disagreeable positives and a positive against every unpleasant negative. In your mind, turn the world on its head." This way of reconciling Christ's teaching and our practice endured for most people so long as he was considered a Demiurge, a God who became man, who lived and suffered but who was quite different from man, a unique creature who was really alien to their difficulties. It had to endure because we were tied by two otherwise irreconcilable facts: we could neither reject his words which were divine, nor could we put them into practice, being ourselves human. Then when Christ's manhood was again accepted, his specific teaching was made even more unreal. It ceased to be fact at all, even "Heavenly fact." As there was no real Heaven or real God, the teaching became pure poetry, preserved and treasured just because it was so beautifully unreal.

It is therefore a good thing for us to be told that the Sermon on the Mount will not work: we have for so long ceased to think of it as an actual instrument: we have for so long valued it only as a "museum piece," like those spinning wheels with which house decorators furnish "old-fashioned" houses, wheels which no one would ever use and which most people doubt were ever used. But if the critics say that this instrument was never intended to be more than a decoration, that Christ was simply "refusing to accept the universe" and waiting for his Father to scrap it and provide another, they go too far. The Sermon on the Mount when it is examined, even by itself, shows that it is more than a gentle defiance, an eloquent veto, a persistent refusal by repeated paradox to take seriously the brutal actual world. Even cursory examination shows that it has a direction of its own. It is not merely a rejection of our values and methods and a challenge to us to find better or to sit back and wait for an apocalyptic smash. It does describe in detail an alternative way. Whether its method prove workable or not, it cannot be dismissed as illogical. It cannot be considered as no more than a series of grandly clever retorts aimed at putting the practical man out of countenance. Its intention is to help him and us to find the true path. It is not simply the image of our common way of living, reversed so as to show a sort of looking-glass world. It is the vision of another world, more real than ours, even if we cannot bring that realm "on earth as it is in Heaven."

Yet if that is so, if we can detect back of these maxims the kind of world which sustains and nourishes such action and such happiness, we are still far from being out of the wood—"that dark wood called the world," as Dante described it. "The Sermon" becomes less "poetic," more rational, logical, consistent—and by so much the more tantalizing, the more heartbreaking. It is not poetry, a lovely satire on the world we call real. It is telling us of an actual place, a positive condition. Poetry, however lofty, never broke anyone's heart. We sigh that its fine fantasy cannot be true, but, as we never let ourselves (once we are grown) put any reliance on the lovely words, we can never be desperately disappointed. What does drive us to despair is when we have dared build on a real hope, have known that there is an actual perfection and have found it unattainable. Which is worse: a mirage of an oasis tantalizing a man who knows that it is a mirage, and therefore sticks to the path he knows and the muddy culvert, or a real fountain cooling the air but not a drop reaching the tongue of the tortured captive dying tethered within a yard of the spring? If we cannot act up to the Sermon on the Mount it were better dismissed as poetry—poetry for the defeated or the sated.

Yet its systematic structure would seem to show that it was made for use. If we look into it we shall see that it is far more argument than oratory. That naturally reawakens hope. What if the Sermon and especially its center, the group of seven Beatitudes, is an argument, but we have failed to realize the logic because this argument is only part of a complete system, the conclusion, the induced consequences of a system? If that were so we should be able to discover the first part, the instructions telling us how the Beatitudes may be made to work, the procedure which will lead to these remarkable consequences.

A previous volume has maintained this thesis. In that book of essays on the Lord's Prayer it has been urged that this Prayer actually gives the basis of training whereby the precepts of the Sermon may become possible, indeed natural. The constructional connection seems inescapable when we put together these two central teachings of Christ. The Prayer must come first. It is making the connection between us and our Father, between the soul and Reality. Until that is done the soul is indeed helpless to live up to the sermon. But once that contact is firmly made there are inevitable consequences. The Beatitudes are the open practice and publication of a secretly prepared proficiency. The Prayer is private. The world thinks prayer to be almost as peculiar as the mutterings of a maniac. Naturally people will only attend when and if there are results from such queer "self-communing." The Sermon is public, social; the consequences of prayer. The long-prepared forces come out into the open. The Beatitudes show the divine policy; the line of action, at last possible to those (but only possible to them) who have become proficients in the life of Prayer. Here we see the deployment of the trained and ranged forces.

The collection of essays on the first part of Christ's system, the Lord's Prayer was called *The Creed of Christ*. For it was argued that in that five-clause prayer we have the minimum hypothesis, the five postulates required for training the human soul. The message of Christ was that the world can be, and can only be, saved by reborn men and that reborn men, men with a transmuted consciousness, a new quality of awareness can only be so remade by two things: First by believing certain basic truths—few but essential, and then by acting on those truths. The Lord's Prayer is a method of training but it is also something more. It starts with us even earlier than that. It shows us how to begin to think that training is worth while and possible. The Lord's Prayer seems to make the minimum irreducible postulates required if we are to alter our characters, to become constantly intentional, really conscious, to "change human nature." Those five demands made of us, those five provisional conclusions on which we must be resolved to work, are as follows: First, that the Ultimate Nature of Reality—whatever appearances may seem to suggest—is not alien from us but is our source, our sustainer and our goal. He is our creator, our providence and our aim. He is our Father because he caused us and loves us. And because Reality is this and no other we are bound therefore to act in accordance with Reality. We must learn from Him how to hallow His name, how to act so that all our behavior will accord with the nature of Reality and none of our deeds or words deny or "take His name in vain." We must further believe that His Kingdom, the state of Being where He is unmistakably manifest is to come "on earth," to all men, as it now is among those who are actually and forever in His full Presence. Thirdly, we must hold that in order that this may come about we can receive a diet, a transforming nourishment whereby we become beings able to live in that Eternal Day. Fourthly, having assimilated that "bread" we believe that by virtue of it we become able at once to be forgiven and to forgive, and on ever wider range and scale until we forgive as God Himself forgives. Fifthly, we believe that though Evil and Omnipotence are a supreme mystery, our Father does not lead us into temptation, but does deliver us and will finally and for good save us from the Evil.

Such are the postulates, the irreducible acts of faith, the minimum of "nobler hypotheses" which must be made and chosen by any human being if he wishes to change human nature. So, and so only, may he ever hope to alter his own nature and then the nature of others by the contagion of the new life in him. And enwrought with these postulates are the instructions for the transmuting training. Put very simply they run: Turn to the hidden Reality who unseen is always at hand. Know Him as God Transcendent, the all Powerful—and God Immanent, God all compassionate—in briefest phrase know Him as your Heavenly Father. Long every moment for His Presence to be manifest to you and to all. Breathe in constantly the atmosphere of That His Presence. Let the sense of His perfect unlimited Fatherhood constantly recover you from all your mistakes. So being constantly restored you, in turn, shall be able increasingly to remedy and cancel the mistakes which His other children, your brethren, make in dealing with you. Realize that as you so live and because you are so living in His Presence, even the occasions of stumbling, those situations in which any possible course seems to lead to some wrong, such circumstances are no longer arising. Your course no longer leads you into dubious situations. Then you will experience as a final unshakable assurance presaging victory, that all Evil is being dissolved by the Presence of the Eternal Light, Who alone is Reality, Potency and Consciousness. With such a training completed the Beatitudes become an inevitable conclusion.

As then the Sermon is here being considered as the Prayer's corollary and these seven essays are a sequel to the five on the Prayer, these are called the Code of Christ. The Prayer gives the power, the Sermon gives the policy. Certainly if the Prayer is the quintessence of all the Creeds, the Sermon may be called the Christian Code. Indeed this title word—code—is trebly apposite. It has three meanings and each of these cover one of the threefold characteristics of the Beatitudes. They are a Law: they are a Loyalty or an obligation and they are a Mystery. The word code is here used in these three senses.

Code in its eldest sense means a system of laws and principles as for example the Emperor Justinian's great codification of Roman Law and the Code Napoléon of French Jurisprudence. In its second sense we use the word to mean a high-minded man's behavior, his conduct and rule of life, the "Law written in his heart" from which he will not deviate for bribe or threat—his code of honor. The third sense of the word code gives the third characteristic of the Beatitudes. They are the Law of God, the principles of Reality: they are also, because we are His children, born of His great nature and being, a law written in our hearts. However hard, however impossible we may find it to act on these laws, to implement them in our present living, yet we know they are true for our hearts respond to them. However defeatist, squalid and treacherous our acts and behavior, we wish that this Great Law might be done; we know it must be right. But, owing to the tragic conflict in our hearts the Beatitudes are a code in the third sense of the word—a message needing decoding; some dispatch of vital importance but compressed, obscure, cryptic. We sense a terrible beauty in these short sayings: we realize that they must hold a secret of such significance that if we could grasp it, for us the world would be transformed. Indeed it would—but there is the rub—who shall read for us the writing, find the key, decode the oracle—who may make these gnomic utterances actually come into gear with our actual lives? Granted that the Prayer told us about our personal preparation, we, who are still striving so to become conditioned, how can we really yet understand this policy, both so majestic and so obscure?

The essays that follow, need it be said, are written by one who dare hardly call himself a beginner, one at the level of sub-servanthood, a creature hardly caught, scarcely "broken." The view which such a semiwild creature has of the Father's House must be scanty and low. Hence for one thing, there will be apparent repetitions in this book of themes which appeared in the reflections on the Lord's Prayer. The Beatitudes—at least from this level—seem to repeat again with vaster scope and significance, phrases initially sounded in the Prayer: for example, the key of the Prayer, Forgiveness, is transposed, it would seem, in the Beatitudes into one even more comprehensive—Mercifulness. Hence, for another thing, more issues, vaster and more confusing, are raised in the Beatitudes. We seem driven to conclude that here we are facing ultimates—for example, the final vision of God, which only appeared in the Prayer by implication and as a result not yet to be attained. In short we have a picture of things in which we are part, but only part of an immense design; where before, in the Prayer, we were the central figure if only as an obstacle to be reduced. This means that certain considerations such as the significance of life as a whole, the destiny of all creatures, the purpose and fate of the universe, have to be considered. The fact that the present writer has attempted to face these issues will not, he hopes, appear to suggest that he thinks that he has solved them or even has contributed anything of value to their solution. All he would hope is that he may perhaps stimulate fresh inquiry into problems which, however difficult, are the inescapable concern of every soul and with which the Beatitudes deal.

Meanwhile the fact remains that we are confronted with a code, and we must see, before we can add any hypotheses or explanatory speculations, how far we can go with the actual words to make agreed common sense, a meaning about which we can all have a preliminary understanding.

The best course, when faced with a code, in this sense of the word, is to start with any part of the message where there occur phrases which we can clearly grasp. So, working from the known to the unknown, from the clear to the hidden, we may gradually learn the language and uncover the meaning.

There is one term which is central in the Beatitudes and it is a term which we all feel that we know intimately, understand fully and rightly and reasonably deserve. Let us start with that. That word is "blessed," or, if we prefer the colloquial synonym, "happy."

# THE CODE OF CHRIST

# I.

## THE PATHWAY TO HAPPINESS

✤✤✤✤✤✤✤✤✤✤✤✤✤✤✤✤✤✤✤✤✤✤✤✤✤✤✤✤✤✤✤✤✤✤✤✤✤✤

There are very few things on which it is possible to get men to agree. Perhaps there is only one thing which all men will agree that they want. That is happiness. Wisdom may be above rubies in value, and yet in the end even it proves vanity, but happiness is always worth while. The Gospels mean good news, we know. We know also that a great deal of them is taken up with other things—the depressing reception given the good news, the almost more depressing muddle and misconceptions made by those who decided, here was good news but it must be the kind of good news that they considered good, it must not be too good to be true. But at the center of the Gospel story there is a core. It is a core in two senses of the word. It is that essence of which everyone who reads them feels when they reach that part—here is the heart of the whole matter, this *is* the Gospel, the Good News. It is also the center—that part of the narrative which experts seem agreed must be as close as we shall ever get to those sudden, short heart-opening sayings, the key words of the Christ. Here are those seed sentences which could sow (and have for near two thousand years sown) new life in the exhausted furrows of man's heart; those brief phrases unweighted with argument but driven home with that irresistible force only belonging to spiritual truth, accepted as true by man because his spirit hungers for them as his body for bread, for they are those creative words, carrying their own undeniable authentication, "proceeding out of the mouth of God."

This core is the so-called Sermon on the Mount, and at the heart of this core, as the germ itself lies in the germ cell, are seven short sentences. Here we are at the essence of the Good News and, it is quite clear on inspection, that the name was not a misnomer. These seven key sentences, it is true, do, all of them, deal with the one thing which actively interests all of us: Happiness. These seven sentences have locked up in them first the vital definitions as to what happiness really is, how to be really happy and then, to each of these definitions, is attached an explanatory reason, telling us why, in each case, happiness is obtained by doing so or being so. Indeed, so comprehensive and extensive are these definitions that we may say that all the rest of the Gospels, all the rest of the New Testament is simply a series of illustrations showing how this strange happiness actually did work as long as the strange reasons were believed in, and how happiness was lost as soon as ordinary reason interfered.

The explanatory reasons are then very necessary, for the Christian church proved, almost at once, how hard it was to resist common sense and act on this divine recipe for happiness. And when we run through the definitions of the Happy, of those who, we are told, are fortunate, it is certainly clear that we do need reasons for thinking that such sorts of people, these seven categories of characters, could even be reasonably comfortable let alone blessed.

In these seven chapters there will be an attempt to view these seven sentences under two considerations. First they will be viewed as a sequel and then as themselves an evolution, a story leading up to the meaning and culmination of Life, the goal of the universe, the end and explanation of Time. They are viewed as a sequel because of the belief that these, the only true happinesses, are made possible by something that has gone before. The demand for happiness has been so constant, the need for it so pressingly and universally felt that had it been at all easily attained surely by now we should have understood how to secure it. Yet in anno Domini 1941 and maybe the year 8000 since the founding of the first civilized city, we don't seem to be getting any closer to happiness—quite the reverse. Evidently then, happiness is not something which simply happens. On the contrary it needs great skill to attain. The Beatitudes deal with happiness, but he who spoke them, though he knew they were the true and lasting felicity, did not imagine that they could be easily achieved. He gave therefore the instructions for reaching the athletic efficiency required to live in this dynamic intensity of spiritual health. Those instructions, as has been said, one believes are contained in the Lord's Prayer. The Beatitudes are then being considered here as a sequel, a story telling us what happens to the people who live the life of the

Lord's Prayer. The seven happinesses are, as it were, a ladder set up on the firm platform made by the five petitions, earnestly asked and fully granted. The seven are taken as a seven-runged ladder because there seems to be apparent in them an evident progression, a rising in height and range, a stepping up from a datum line and base, from a state well known to all of us to a final station at which man passes out of our vision, entering fully into the presence of the Eternal.

Whatever may be the ultimate goal we need have no doubt that the foot of this ladder rests well at our level. Indeed when we note where it starts we may think it starts altogether too low. Granted that seeing God is the highest happiness, if a little too lofty for us now, a super-happiness—the first clause, the starting class of those that are said to be the happy, is surely sub-happy. It may be hard to imagine someone incessantly, obliviously happy just because he sees God. It is certainly harder to imagine those first named in this list of the blessed as being happy at all. As has just been said we require reasons to inform us why people in such states are to be congratulated. Let us then run through the list, run our eye up the whole ladder and get the general impression. Then, when we are no longer in danger of losing sight of the ladder because of the rungs, we can look and handle each of them in turn. Right Knowledge, a right sense of general direction, must come before Right Resolve and Right Effort. Blessed are the poor in spirit; blessed are they that mourn; blessed are the meek; are those who hunger and thirst after righteousness; are the merciful; the peacemakers: the pure in heart. Two things stand out at once at this cursory glance. The series is certainly a ladder, a sequence: and it certainly starts at a very modest, indeed we might say a depressed and depressing level and mounts to something lofty if, from our common-sense standpoint, more than a little airy.

You will notice that in the arrangement of sequence of this sevenfold key classification one change has been made. In the series as Matthew gives it the peacemakers hold the final place. I think we can see the probable reason for this when we glance through the list of reasons why each class, each level is to be considered fortunate. Here are the reasons: the poor in spirit are blessed because theirs is the Kingdom of Heaven; those that mourn because they shall be comforted; the meek for they shall inherit the earth; the hungry and thirsty for righteousness because they will get fully what they want. The merciful also are to get what they give. The peacemakers, however, go a step further. No doubt they get peace, but they also get a new rank and recognition; they are called the Children of God. The pure in heart also are not paid back in their own coin. They do not simply grow in integrity. They can exchange what they have earned. The achieved sense of complete singleness, the entire unity of their being, the supreme wholeness, of which the highest health, the firmest sanity are only aspects, this when won, great as it is, can be exchanged for something supremely greater, the seeing of God, the realization of Reality.

[5]

Now Matthew was writing for people who, whatever they lacked, believed in God. Their weakness was that they didn't believe enough that God cared for them. The good Jew of that time had with great effort built up in his mind the idea of God Transcendent. Clinging to that, acutely anxious to prevent that high faith from becoming again contaminated by lower notions, the Jew lost sight of God Immanent. Putting his idea high and safe above the touch of profane hands he found that he had put it where he himself could hardly keep any touch with it. He strained after his soul's desire not realizing that, though that desire would always be beyond, and, safely beyond, intellectual limitation; it was always nigh the seeker for it was in the heart itself prompting the search. Hence the climax for Matthew and his readers would not be so much in seeing God. "I shall see Him but not nigh: I shall behold Him but far off," had said the unwilling prophet Baalam. God must be seen in the end, for He stands at the end of every road, at the close of every event. Like the sky He is the unsurpassable limit; He is the ultimate range and horizon on which finally every eye must rest. "Whither then shall I go from Thy presence? If I go down into hell Thou art there also!"

The Jew did not think of that vision as other thinkers as pure as he thought of it, those thinkers who held to the two great antinomic thoughts—God Transcendent and God Immanent—and would let neither go, those thinkers who therefore held that by what we see we are actually ourselves trans-

[6]

formed. So Matthew would naturally feel that the climax was not merely seeing God—"while on the furtherest limit far withdrawn God made Himself an awful rose of Dawn." The climax would be returning like Moses from the mountain, with face resplendent, carrying the tables of the New Law, returning with manifest authority as the children of God, as those who have the power to bring peace on earth. The mystics and all those lovers and contemplators of God who have clung both to His Immanence and Transcendence have, however, had an idea, a revelation which to the Jew would have seemed blasphemous. It is that when we see God, as we are transformed, we, as separate self-seeking wills are completely radiated away—we become God. This is not blasphemy. The little ego does not swagger about saying, "I am God." As each soul yields and is transmuted there is heard still another whisper in the leaves of the Tree of Life, still another murmur in the ripples of the infinite Ocean of Being swelling that eternal creative word, "There is none but God: He alone is all." So, as our age supremely needs the belief in God in Himself, and as we know that seeing God can and does alone sufficiently transform man so that the world can be transformed, the culmination of the Beatitudes is for us—Blessed are the singlehearted for they see God.

But that is the high goal; at present, for us, among the clouds. At our earth level it really hardly matters whether we are to be full children of God or to enter a state beyond even that. Some mystics think that in the blaze and splendor of the Eternal Light, gazing at that splendor, radiated through by that Essence of all Being, we shall still be able to reflect on how wonderful it feels for us limited beings to be present in the unlimited Life. Others say that if temporal beauty in sound and sight can make us utterly oblivious of ourselves, how shall we remain unfused and double, reflecting, recollecting, comparing, noting and commenting, when we face and are swept by that Incomparable Instantaneity in which every experience of loveliness is gathered up in one overwhelming Present. Such speculations are good for us to listen to now and then. They keep our spirits stretched, as the stir of their mother moving keeps kittens, when still blind, yet able to begin exercising themselves by crawling clumsily toward what they cannot yet see. But in the perspective of our rudimentary outlook these farthest horizons can hardly be distinguished. Children of God or United with God—such a question is like that supposed to have been asked by an anxious layman at the conclusion of the astronomer's lecture. "Had the astronomer said the universe would last a thousand million million years or had he said it would only last a mere thousand million?" On being told that the higher figure had been proposed the inquirer's acute anxiety was assuaged. So are most of us when we anxiously ask about our final station; as separate or united? We must climb, climb to an immense height before we can even hope to distinguish between such transcendent qualities.

# II.

## PURGATION

### *The Emptying of the Self*

✛✛✛✛✛✛✛✛✛✛✛✛✛✛✛✛✛✛✛✛✛✛✛✛✛✛✛✛✛✛✛✛✛✛✛✛✛✛✛✛✛✛✛

*"Blessed are the poor in spirit: for theirs is the Kingdom of Heaven."*

Let us then start without further delay at the first rung. We have seen sufficiently the ladder's direction, slant and grade. Now we must approach it, get our hands on the foot of it which reaches down to our level, set about the hard and exhausting work of actually mounting it. Yet perhaps it was not a waste of time to get quite firmly in our mind's eye the extraordinary altitude to which it reaches, for, as we have seen, it certainly starts depressingly low. Few things awake more quickly the impatience and contempt of young climbers, setting out with a good guide to conquer their first big peak, than the absurd saunter at which the veteran sets out, as well as his patient apparent fussiness in inspecting all the gear. Yet this is the way won by hard experience: it is not due to a stubborn wish to suppress the young. To skip the early stages is only to have to face far longer and more discouraging delays, checks, breakdowns and repairs later and in less favorable circumstances.

[9]

Starting then at the beginning we have seen that the Beatitudes begin, as it were, where the Lord's Prayer leaves off. The Lord's Prayer was comprehensively concerned with one thing, with getting us empowered to be part of one embracing concept. That five-clause prayer is wholly taken up with the one idea of the Kingdom of God, from "Thy Kingdom come" to the culminating, "For Thine is the Kingdom." And straight away here, as though there were no pause between the Prayer and the Blessing, we start once again with the Kingdom. The Prayer was to train us to become members. Here we find ourselves being told about the actual inhabitants and citizens of the Kingdom. We are told of their nature, their character. This first clause of the Beatitudes is then of the liveliest interest to us who have been concerned with the instructions given in the Prayer, for the story is being carried on. We are being told no longer of those who have to get ready and of those who are getting ready but of those who have actually arrived. We are given a description of the people who already inhabit and possess that crowning position and state toward which the whole Lord's Prayer points and longs.

Who are they? Surely avatars, first magnitude saints, men of power, women of charm (saintly of course but authentic charm), healthy, radiant, magnetic, influential, authoritative, nobly successful. The Kingdom's full citizens must be types of that sort, characters that we all want to be and often, when we have time, try to be. But there's the depressing thing about this start, the rub at the very first rung, the rather dismal paradox at the first step. There can be no doubt about it: the poor in spirit are to be held blessed because theirs specifically is the Kingdom of Heaven.

Yes, this is a stumbling block rather than a rung, this very first clause. And that seems the reason why efforts have been made, for a very long time, to cut it and make it less awkward to our notions. It has been revised so as to read—blessed are the poor, just those without money, not those without the three great Gs—go, guts and grit. But why do we think it is better to cut off that final definition of final poverty, poorness in spirit? Why do we think it better to say—blessed are the poor, the poor people who have not got money? First of all because we do think, both the good and the bad of us, that to be poor in what we call goods is the true and ultimate poverty and disaster. It is interesting and instructive to see how we use that word poor, for its use reveals where we think real good to lie. "Poor so-and-so," we say, and when we say it perfunctorily all we mean is that we are looking down on the person we are gossiping over. Probably we are calling them poor because they are so bitter and backbiting in their gossip about us. "Poor so-and-so" with a deeper sincerity and almost alarm in our voice, means that they are ill, probably going to have a risky operation—something that might happen to us. "Poor dear so-and-so" was always said with an almost propitiary sympathy, for that phrase and tone used always to mean that the poor dear was dead. Yet none of these "poors" really carried off the palm. None of their poverties were, in our eyes, poorness par excellence. Our common speech and phraseology, which is always betraying what our real values actually are, defines quite clearly what we mean by being poor. Poverty, essential real poverty, is just not having money.

So when Christ said something about the poor being blessed we were sure what he meant. A moment's reflection on his words and character makes it quite clear that his notions about what manner of lack made a man poor were quite different from ours. If he had been thinking mainly of cash poverty then his specific concern would have shown in the type of recompense whereby the lack was to be made good, whereby the recompensed were to be shown to be blessed, made happy. On this reading, the passage should run: Blessed are the poor for they shall be made rich. But the actual explanation as to why the poor are to be held fortunate is not that. It is a strange reason, so strange that we shall have to come back and study it again a little later. For the poor, to whom Christ refers, are to be held happy not because they will get the goods, not because they will inherit the earth—quite a different and later class gets that—but because they already have their consolation. Theirs, we are told, is that state, mysterious but important to Christ above all other states and conditions—the Kingdom of Heaven.

But we want so much to believe that he really shared our standards, and that his aim was no more than to make us more effectively what we are, that we urge that here he must have meant what we mean. "Look what he said about the rich," we say. "He disliked them as much as we do!" But did he? It looks more as though he pitied them as fools. "It is just too bad for you," he remarked to them, "because you have had your consolation. You call money your means and it is, in a way, but then you men of means are always failing by your means to get to the end, the goal." The big business man who was so busy expanding his business that he didn't know he had worn himself out at it and was going to die that very night leaving everything unfinished; of him Christ spoke with an understanding which reveals the poor fellow, who thought himself the very devil of a realist, as a dreamy fool. Christ says that God speaking to this foolish creature does not threaten him with punishment but questions the fool according to his folly: "You will be dead tomorrow and then your heart will be broken because, your heart being where your treasure is, who do you think will be playing ducks and drakes with your hoards and cashing out on your absurd self-denials?" Christ loved the rich young man. He did not despise him as a hypocritical prig as most of us would have done. He understands that the rich need the Kingdom as much as any one and, in a way, with all their energy, are blindly, blunderingly trying to find it. He goes up to such and says, "'Friend, you, like all mankind, require to enter the Kingdom. The gate is small, though not impassable. But you will never get through it with all that impedimenta on your back. Slip it off, as a loaded camel goes down on its knees and is unburdened. Then you will push through as easily as the ordinary man; for under all your caparison and baggage you are the ordinary man."

We must then take care not to make the attainment of this, the first and fundamental stage of happiness, falsely easy by the trick of making out that you can be admitted among the Blessed if only you have no cash. We must remind ourselves that the cant of today is always to excoriate the cant of yesterday. Our grandparents were smug about their cash and dull-conscienced in their use of it. We are smug about our social conscience. Dr. Johnson, who could often put his heavy finger right upon sham moralizing, remarked that men were seldom so innocently engaged as when they were making money. He did not mean that they were doing good, but he was backing up another eighteenth-century doctor moralist, Dr. Watts, who remarked that, "Satan finds some mischief still for idle hands to do." Money-making may often be mischievous but it is almost as often a restricted mischief. Other human activities as the love for power—of which money-love is only the weakest of its fingers—the love of revenge, the love of malice, these are almost unlimited evils. So when people say, "It is just social escapism that adds those words 'poor in spirit' to the first Beatitude," we must challenge that attempted pruning of the key phrase. If a man is only poor in cash, further if a man has only made himself poor in money, will he really have rid himself of the other ruthless cravings, cravings which batten on his neighbor? Will he not find, has it not been found, that the ego, driven out of its holding and cover that it had in its possessions, takes refuge, doubly roots itself and doubly becomes aggressive in its pretensions? Conversely, if a man has really faced up to the root of his anti-social nature, if he has seen that it is the ego with its three tentacles: its addictions, its bodily greeds; its possessions, its economic graspingness; its pretensions, its envious craving for exclusive recognition—it is the self which is the source of all the varieties of evil; then the base cause being destroyed, all surface manifestations wither and fall.

The love of money is only one of the ego's manifestations. Cut back only that tendril and the stem will sprout two in its place. The whole plant must be extirpated. Hercules found when wrestling with the infernal giant Antaeus that every time he threw him down, the brute only came up stronger. He saw that the monster by touching the earth, his mother, always recovered all his violence. The hero therefore had to snatch his antagonist up bodily and, only when he was torn from every contact, could his diabolic strength be crushed out of him. So with any vice—they are all allied and basically linked with the ego. Get rid of it and the love of money must fail. The passion to acquire has no longer any root and atrophies. Fail to go so deep and, however much you may prune the one spray of bramble, the thorn bush will grow lustier; and soon, do what you will, even that branch, which you thought you had lopped to the socket, is flourishing boldly again in your face.

The dictators of today all began by denouncing wealth, by appealing to the little man's envy and fear of the big man's display and power. But already some of the dictators are not merely arbitrary in power; they are unlimited in supplies and one or two are beginning actually to show the inevitable completion of the cycle, the inevitable full expression and flowering of the root-ego which has been growing underground all the time. A man like Goering already has yielded to vulgar display; Hitler to fantastic building worthy of the insane Leopold of Bavaria. Eugene Lyons says that Stalin has six houses. It is certainly natural, certainly to be expected, certainly less malignant a symptom than killing one's associates, though, indicative of our obsession with money, ostentatious expenditure on oneself now seems more shocking than massacre.

Of course we must doubt all root cutting that does not lead to leaf and branch fading and falling. If the man who says he has reduced the ego still is assertive, and still clings to his toys, then we know that the operation has been a sham. He went into the hospital but ran out at the back door omitting the painful session on the operating table. But it must be repeated the real operation effects a cure, the only radical cure. With the ego enucleated, the love of money goes, not with subconscious unwillingness, because it yielded under the pressure of that "white mail" which we call social conscience, but willingly. A practical test is to see how the man who has got rid of this grip really feels about it. If he feels noble like a man who lost an arm in saving a family from fire, then we see that he really still wants back his possessions, and, as the soul is much more like a lobster than is the body, sooner or later, if the occasion offers, he will grow again the limb and tentacle he lopped. For he cut it not because he wanted to be free but because other people said such ostentatious outgrowths were no longer worn by the most admired character. If on the other hand the man who has relieved himself of otiose money, feels, not amputated but rather like one who, with improved health, finds he can go about without mufflers and crutches—does not feel noble or fine in any way, only that he was a fool not to have gone fit and free sooner—when this happens the root is really cut, the undesirable growth and fruit are gone for good.

So we see it is superficial nonsense, the typical topical illusion, to say being poor in spirit is an escapist's gloss, a forgery to lead us away from the real hard thing—just to be poor in our money-obsessed sense. "It's so easy," say these people, "to be poor in spirit. It simply means being poor in a Pickwickian sense, which means not being poor at all." A moment's thought shows however that that very charge of escapism is itself escapism. Above have been given examples of the way in which the world's leaders, who made much of their appeal by attacking wealth and lived simply while rising, now having risen to full power are becoming ostentatious also. When that does not happen, poverty itself becomes an ostentation. The arrogance of the austere party member has been social reform's worst advocate, its poorest propaganda; the pride of the mendicant, the greatest stumbling block on the road to God. True, he is good and, in a way, sincere; but does anyone really trust him in the true sense of wanting to be with him and like him?

If then any poverty, voluntary or involuntary, which stops short of poverty of spirit, is going to fail even to adjust economic inequalities, we must look into this the fundamental purgation. A glance reveals why it is so good, so acid-cleaning. It eats right into the ego's hypocritical defenses just because this kind of poorness has in it no glamour, no drama, no histrionic appeal. Just the description of the other virtues bring a flush to our cheeks. "How I wish I were brave, heroic." And how easy it is for us, if we ever manage to display these less fundamental virtues, to boast discreetly about what we have done. We own that perhaps on that occasion we were generous to a fault or carried courage to the limit of rashness or were too nobly proud. We confess that we cannot help ourselves—that is the way we are made. "If it be a sin to covet honor then am I the most offending man alive." We own we may be sinners but we feel no twinge of disgrace in such failings. On the contrary we are clearly elated that we can both be praised by others for what we have done and also get a second dose of praise by declaring that we fear that the virtue we have shown may have been so excessive as to be censurable by God even if commended by man.

Now look at poverty of spirit. Why, the very word brings a chill. The glow of enthusiasm is gone. The specific Christian and spiritual virtues, as Santayana pointed out, we have never really admired, let alone practiced. The pagan virtues we praise. They are our real ethics. "Here's the man who, holding the gate, singlehanded killed a hundred foes." "Here, the man who a hundred times with cheerful lack of resentment or defensiveness has let his face be smacked." Which statement, which type of courage gives us that instantaneous reaction of admiration? Our hearts betray us. The quickened beat is involuntary applause. We cannot help ourselves, or if we wish to be accurate we have not helped ourselves, for no one is free at the moment of action. We think the spiritual virtues anemic, ghostly. "Thou hast conquered, O pale Galilean, the world hath turned grey with thy breath." Our hearts echo that cry and so we have allowed to come back a state of things which openly declares that it only stands for animal virtues.

That is because we cling to the ego. We would be anything but mean and insignificant, pusillanimous, a poor mean-spirited little creature. We wince from the words, we shrink from the description as we shrink from being dabbed and sponged with a dank dishcloth. What taunt makes us wince most from being described as religious? Not that religion is dangerous, a risky psychological adventure, or apt to get you into trouble with your friends or the community, or even that religion is superstitious, too given to fantasy, too daring in its speculations, too careless with its poetic license to check up on all its fine emotional phrases. No, what really gives us pause when we think of being definitely classed with devout people is the fear that we shall be thought weak; ineffectual, poor creatures who because they have failed with man would cover up their incompetence by taking up with God. "Just look at the people who are religious! Did you ever find one of them who could have been a real success in the world? One and all, they're an anemic lot." That taunt has drawn many a good lover of his fellow man (perhaps loving his fellow man more than he loved God) into counterattack, into angry reaction, away from true Christianity with its specific but intensely difficult technique of dynamic meekness, to that so-called Christianity which advocates all the virtues save this fundamental virtue.

The fear of being thought a fool—a spiritless fool for Christ's sake—has led to many intelligent and vigorous minds leaving Christianity for Chestertonianity.[1] "God," cries the inner man, "I can't stand being called a lily-livered fool and by men who haven't either my heart or brain. I'll teach them a man can be both a Christian and a champion. I'll champion God. My counterattack will

[1] Jerome, who suffered from ill-repressed pride, heard in a dream the guardian angels of Paradise tell him that he was not really a Christian but a Ciceronian. The same vice haunts religion today and in some form it must always haunt mankind: the desire to be stylish even in one's humility, dignified in one's disgrace, to wear the rue of one's conversion with a difference from the common convert, to make self-sacrifice look smart. It was Cicero with his rich style and unreal philosophy who tempted the first Latin Christian scholars. It is a Chesterton who with his verbal cleverness today has offered a similar escape from the reality into rhetoric, from self-naughting to counterattack.

make them find me—and my religion of course—no weak thing unworthy of their steel but highly formidable. When I have done with them I'll be able to cry with Browning's Bishop Blougram and in defense of Christ, 'You see we need not fear for your contempt.' We demonstrate, by turning you inside out, that it was just because we are a deal more clever than you that we became Christians. The spiritual life is just too clever and smart for any but lively fellows such as we." That of course is a way, a common way now, of trying both to find God and keep our self-respect. It is doubtful whether it does either. It is certain it makes no converts. It never can win one soul to true religion, to the selfless love of God and the selfless love of man. For the whole thing, it is painfully plain, is not a counterattack made by us on the irreligious. On the contrary it is a completely successful ambushing of our own souls, a completely successful counterattack made by the ego. So it recovers entirely its possession of the soul which was in danger of deliverance.

So we see two things are plain: the first is why poverty of spirit is so much more searching than mere money poverty—because poverty of spirit is the root and cause, money poverty merely a symptom. The second is why being poor in spirit has to come first, before any other of the great virtues and powers and blessings. It is fundamental, the *sine qua non* of any true dynamic spirituality. That is why all real and truthful trainers of the soul, the great saints, the Friends of God as well as the Sons of God, the spirits who produced in themselves and in others actual spiritual power (not clever argument which silences, but inspiration which convinces; not coercion but lasting conversion)—one and all these trainers bent their power to naught the self. In this our time when Friends of God are few and far between, when the records of the Sons of God we have reinterpreted to the level of our understanding (for "man imputes himself"—he must), we can hardly believe such teaching, such news. It cannot be true that the ego itself must go, for then surely nothing would be left? The answer is an old one: "We do err, not knowing the scriptures or the power of God." But surely self-respect is the only way to save a man? Again an awkward quotation answers us: "He who would save his self must lose his self." That seems fatal to us; just an invitation to suicide or, at best, neurosis. But that is because we have assumed for so long there could be nothing beyond this present notion of myself. The ego, my strangulated pocket of consciousness, that is finality, that is all. As God is just my good will, there is no real help or object outside myself.

Yet even without calling in God, or believing that He exists, we need not remain confined in that starved and childish notion of psychology which materialism attempted to construct. If we stand on no more than the obvious rational fact that the mind is the unmovable basis (because no proof can unprove the mind that is required to prove the proof), we can begin to realize that the mind can have functions and developments which transcend physical uses, that the ego is only an aspect of the whole psyche. Then from that base we can begin to explore the psychology of the saints, begin to see sense in what they say about naughting the self, and why by that naughting they produced supercharacters, men and women of specific spiritual power. Buddha who had a protestant dread of superstition, a Hebrew reverence against mentioning the name of God put the essentials of this, the minimal adequate psychology, in a memorable phrase: "The Self is the Lord of the self." In other words— within you if you will seek and give all to find it, is the Eternal Spirit. He is the goal and the way out of that temporary restriction of consciousness which we call the ego. With a poverty-stricken notion of what consciousness actually is, naturally I am sure that the ego cannot be a phase, must be the only possible end. I may work to improve the ego, to get rid of its faults, but surely it is just madness to get rid of it. The poor in spirit, the naughted selves, however, are not mad though they may be daring— no more mad, but as daring as the first circumnavigators who said, amid a chorus of mockery, protest and dismay, "We will sail on till we find continents which must be under our feet. We will sail on till, from persistently leaving everything behind us, we will find ourselves coming back home again." This fundamental Beatitude is in a single phrase an entire description of the soul's circumnavigation—or, if we like a chemical simile better than a geographic—of the soul's transmutation. It is not to be sent tumbling over the edge of the world into the void, the abyss. It is not to be annihilated. The soul is to be released into its next and right kingdom and condition—the Kingdom of Heaven.

So self-naughting is necessary, as an essential part of the evolution of things. The two parts of this first Beatitude, this first station of Happiness, are complementary. The poor in spirit possess the Kingdom of Heaven not as a rest, a relief and reward after the very devil of a time. Heaven is not a blessed contrast, all the more appreciated because of the ghastly condition one had to get oneself into in order to qualify. Heaven is being without an ego. *That* was the hell, that is the hell, that is what is making the world hellish, and it is the loss of the ego that brings Heaven here. Even a little less egotism means a little of heaven now. Yes, it is hard to believe. "Is that all that's wrong?" we say after a moment's reflection. "Is that all that's needed to put things right?" Yes, but it is so much that, rather than attempt it, we have tried every other way. We have tried liquidating nearly every other cause and person save this thing in ourselves. There is no doubt that Christ taught that this was all that was necessary, that each of us could do it now, yet that it was so difficult (because we are both so willfully blind and blindly weak) that we might never succeed in doing it in our entire lives, that it might never be done by mankind until the End of the Age. For look at the tense which he uses in the verb linking up the person and the place, the character and the environment, the type and the habitat. It is not the future tense, though that rules on all other rungs of this ladder. Though the further types, we are told, do by acting earn a further condition, by becoming something they qualify to go on to further position; here, at the first rung and step, that is not so. In this primal Beatitude the present tense is used.

The two reasons for this the saints and mystics have made quite clear. The first we have seen. Hell is a place composed of completely egotistic persons. There is no other hell and all the ranges and degrees of misery can be exactly gauged and calibrated by noting the amount of ego that is present. When the ego dominates wholly in everyone then you have pandemonium and homicidal frenzy, persecution mania, insane suspicion, insane cruelty, a state toward which parts of the world have actually now gone closer than our grandparents would have thought any people could, outside an asylum. When the ego has been checked but not resolved, then we find private suspicions, miseries, complaints and hidden hatreds. When it has begun to be eliminated then we find it only lurking in corners of the mind, in irrational worry, oversensitiveness and mind-body distresses.

Sometimes, indeed many times, many good people stop at that third stage. They think they have done all that can be done. There, then, is great need of accurate and full knowledge. They do not know that they must and can get rid of the ego completely. Once we realize that God alone is pure Being then we understand that if only we can be empty of ourselves, that self which makes us ignore this fact, God does the rest—we are instantaneously filled with the Invisible Reality the moment we get rid of the visible sham. It is only when the glass tube has had all the air that filled it exhausted out of it and contains a vacuum that then the current can run through it and produce X rays—that intense light-invisible which can both see through that which is opaque to our eyes and radically change our flesh, though we cannot feel even the faintest glow as it falls on us. Owing to this spiritual ignorance, through lack of knowledge of the further ranges of psychological evolution, great numbers of good people have failed to understand this, the full hope and promise of the Gospel. You can know the moment you have really and fully gotten rid of the ego. You will not have to feel your soul all over to find whether it is whole—perfect honesty, perfect purity, perfect love. You will know that it is whole, as an instantaneous, complete feeling tells you you are well. You will feel immediately the peace of God, the perfect trust in God, the joy of God. You will know you are in heaven.

That brings us to the second reason why this first Beatitude uses the present tense. It uses it because, as Eckhart puts it, the opening of the door, your escaping out of the suffocating prison of the ego, and God's entering, the King and the Kingdom coming to you, are one and the same act, an instantaneous transaction and reciprocation. That small medieval mystic guidebook called *Theologia Germanica,* looking at what we are, says, "Nothing burns in hell but the ego." Ramakrishnan, the nineteenth-century Indian saint, looking at what we become, says, "Bliss begins that moment the ego dies." But if Heaven is just emptying oneself of the ego and then God must enter, as certainly as air follows and fills each fresh hollow the tunneler makes with his spade, then why can't we be in heaven at a stroke?[2] Just because we can't open up instantly what has been sealed up so persistently.

We can only open up by inches, and, as far as we can make the door give we get. God enters, we have the Kingdom, precisely as far as we choose to let Him in. He can only enter proportionately as we empty out our egos. It is a slow business for most of us. Though every instant we give and every inch we yield is instantaneously filled, though we know we have been given some of what we want, we are slow in taking more. Why? Spinoza's question gets near the dark reason. "We can will, but can we will to will?"

No doubt, as mentioned above, part of our silly slowness is due to ignorance. Few people today know much about this, the further evolution; the evolution of consciousness, about the ladder of Happiness. The way has become lost. Hence many good people, as we have seen, think they have arrived, think the door is wide open, think they are breath-

[2] In Zen Buddhism there are two great schools of practice: the one is the "sudden" school, believing in conversion, conversion like a thunder clap or a box on the ear—indeed this actual method of sudden precipitation of conviction is sometimes used, or a sudden seemingly pointless phrase (the Kohan). Compare: Augustine's conversion through "Tolle: Lege." The other school teaches the opposite way, saying, "You go to Buddha by inches."

ing full deep the breath of heaven when as a matter of fact they are still gasping like asthmatics. No wonder we don't make a very striking propagandist impression on ordinary people who have their doors tight shut and peer at us through their fogged windows. No wonder we ourselves often feel more like forlorn hopes, with the accent distinctly on the adjective, men working in a gathering twilight rather than those stepping out into the dawn. No wonder we often say to ourselves as one of Aldous Huxley's young well-read heroes remarks after his first love affair, "Is that all!" Is this courageous lip-bitten patience, this uncomplaining humility, is this the Kingdom of Heaven of the poor in spirit?

Thank Heaven no! Thank Heaven what we took to be the last chapter was anything but. Full poorness of spirit ( we must use paradox to describe it), full freedom from the ego, full possession of and by that full open consciousness which lies above and beyond the last crags and clouds of the ego, that is utterly beyond both humility and patience for it is beyond and free of all effort and all restraint. Do not mistake me: humility and patience cannot be dispensed with at the start. You must do a thing painfully, yes and badly, before you can do it easily and well. But in the end, when the jambed door swings full open, then there is no longer any grimness or grit. Heaven, there is never a doubt, Heaven is happiness; and happy, as we can never know happiness until we are so emptied and refilled, are and are alone those that have been poured out and had poured into them the Eternal Light. Patience at best is sweetly dogged. It just knows it can stick us out, tire out our perversity and ill will. At a cost it can by its dynamic nonviolence wear down our violence. But that, thank God, is not the last word in life nor the final triumph of love—a wrestling match wherein by throwing in their last ounce of good will, their years of accumulated persistent kindness, the patient keep their desperate hold and, gasping with exhaustion, the saint and his quarry the sinner, the holy retriever and the wild beast lie saved, but by the skin of the teeth. That is fine training but it is not a proficient performance. No, when the ego has gone, when the real and holy poverty is won, then the characteristic is not a vigilant patience but rather something which looks far more like a cheerful indifference. Much of our grim patience is because we are afraid we shall lose and are afraid of losing. That fear, and indeed all fear, is one of the signs (not the only one) of a still lurking, still unreduced ego. We are anxious not to fail in facing that crisis, in helping that tough case, in making the person here and now not miss his opportunity of seeing the Light.

Christ gave us light on the kind of attitude and frame of soul we should achieve and will achieve when we are emptied and refilled. Close to the Beatitudes, perhaps as a flashing summary he cried, "In short, be perfect, be unlimited as your Father in Heaven is Perfect, is unlimited, inexhaustible." And then, having drawn the line at infinity, having said the sky is the limit, he gives, in another single phrase the character of the Infinite. What is His outstanding and yet all embracing attribute? He is kind and He is not carefully kind—we might say rather He is indiscriminately, effortlessly generous. He is to be thought of as the wide inexhaustible Heaven overarching all, needing nothing of any, giving everything, sun and rain and radiation, light and moisture, to all below regardless of their deserts. It is some such inexhaustible generosity, careless, infinite, unattached, uncalculating, that those in the Kingdom enjoy. They do not have any longer to budget and estimate and make patient balances— their resources against the world's need. They have ceased to have limits—they cannot be drained and run dry because they are no longer little self-contained cisterns. They are simply wide-open sluices letting in the sea, unobstructed apertures letting past the light.

We cling from letting ourselves go, letting ourselves rise and be carried away into that vast expanse of unrestricted Liberty—the freedom of the Children of God. Why? A kind of timid ignorance holds us back and that timid ignorance, like most shyness, is at bottom a form of subtle pride. True, struggling to the last gasp with evil is very exhausting but surely it is gallant too. To win by the skin of one's teeth, to win singlehanded is agonizing, but then think of the honor. So there, still smugly ensconced, is the ego quietly remaking, out of its apparent sacrifice and elimination, a still deeper burrow where it may sit out our reforming zeal and, when we are outwardly successful, morally famous, busily engaged in making others good, out it will dart and repossess itself of all our being which we thought was delivered forever.

That is an all too common biographical sketch of the vicious-circled good. Starting out to be rid of the self by giving it to God they end by giving themselves, all their simpler passions, to a bloated development of themselves, through spiritual pride. The full saint is curiously unnoticeable. It is half-saints who are great characters. The characteristic of the holy is not that they are outstanding but understanding. Singularity, peculiar distinctiveness, said a mystic, is a vice God hates extremely. We may say of the consecrated, "Oh, if the stature of the soul but showed how he would tower." But it does not show. Increase the intensity of visible light. It does not become more dazzling, it passes into the ultra-violet and becomes wholly invisible. Buddhists say, "Do you want to be invisible? Very well, manage never to think of yourself for two years and after that no one will ever notice you." Do we want to be as invisible, intangible, all-sustaining as the air? Everyone who is of the Spirit, Christ tells us, has just that unemphatic pervasive quality. Do we want to be as unnoticeable as the Heavens? The spirit of our Father, Christ tells us, is as comprehensive, as unperceived, as unassertive.

And as little as complete poor-spiritedness is, finally, a patient, enduring thing, so is it no longer what we call humility. For humility is still making an effort to keep deflated, trying not to begin to swell with blisters of resentment when trodden on, or, worse, neglected; trying to avoid that flatulence of self-satisfaction that bubbles inside as long as a scrap of ego is left, like bacteria, to swarm over and ferment any good act. Humility is still thinking about itself. Full, true selflessness, that state so high and real that our poor ego-centered, ego-infested vocabulary can only state this supreme positive by negatives, has no self to suppress. All its being is uncoiled, unwrapped. The little sour eddy swirling round its petty collection of dust and garbage has been unfolded and swept clear in that River of Light and Life which Dante saw as the Life of God as manifested in Time.

Such then is the promise of the very first Beatitude. God is not slow in giving. At the start we may have all—all we can hold. Then, we may ask, why does the ladder have further rungs? For two reasons. The first and simplest is that what has been inwardly attained may now be made manifest and available to and for all. The self has been opened to the Light. It must now open its other side, the side that adjoins its fellow man. The remainder of the Beatitudes have their consequences, as we have seen, placed in the future. They are of the nature of an agenda, of work to be done. They are the working out and applying in Time what has taken place instantaneously in the deep spark of the soul, when, by letting fall its shroud, it becomes one with the One Light. The second reason is that the seven-stepped ladder of the Beatitudes resembles that other famous ascent to Understanding and Deliverance—the Eightfold Path of Buddha. They both have this important feature in common: though the steps are a series and an ascent, yet, in another sense, all the steps lie side by side, that is, we have to make some start on all of them at once. Take the two extremes in the ladder of Blessedness—this first one, the poor-spirited and the last one, the singlehearted, and the two reasons for considering these two classes blessed, the being in the Kingdom of God and the seeing of God; ultimately these two are the same thing. As soon as we are quite emptied of the lower self, freed of the ego, immediately we are singlehearted. We are in Heaven because we see God. But we must practice this freedom from the self, we must make it actual in every aspect of our life before what has been given us becomes fully ours. It must be not merely a matter of our wills, but of our subconscious wills, yes, right out to our reveries and right down to our reflexes. We must, by acting on this new freedom, by continually drawing on the Eternal Life, which now is free to flow through us, learn to make it deliver us not merely from our private self-will; but soul, mind, body, must no longer have any frontiers—the divine vitality must pour through us to the souls, minds and bodies of every other living being.

So we must turn to the further Beatitudes. As we master each we shall bring back some further grasp and hold upon the first. Now therefore we must immediately examine the second. We must inquire how and why it is—because we have begun to learn of poverty of spirit, and as far as we have learned, are in the Kingdom—how and why it is that we can mourn and can be comforted.

# III.

## PROFICIENCY—i

### *The True Diagnosis*

✤✤✤✤✤✤✤✤✤✤✤✤✤✤✤✤✤✤✤✤✤✤✤✤✤✤✤✤✤✤✤✤✤✤✤✤✤✤✤✤✤

*"Blessed are they that mourn: for they shall be comforted."*

We must repeat that reckoning, so as to take our bearings at this new next level. For certainly our position, strange on the first rung, is becoming paradoxical at the second. We have been made free of the Kingdom by being shown the way out of our asphyxiating prison, the ego—and in consequence? In consequence we are to be able to mourn. That is certainly an odd, a very odd conclusion. Conclusions, deductions as strange as this, when made by authorities as great as the preacher of that mountain sermon, deserve and repay the most careful thought.

The first thing to recall is that the world's two greatest teachers, the Light of Asia and the Light of the World, both prefaced their gospel by this same specific introduction. Not a very prepossessing preface we may think, but the fact remains that both these supreme vehicles of the spirit emphasize that sorrow is the celestial beginning of joy, sorrow is the first word of the Good News.

Perhaps it may seem a mere accident that Buddha

[ 34 ]

foretold the teaching of Christ. Was not the Indian simply a tired-eyed pessimist who saw nothing in life but misery? If that were so, was not the Great Galilean also a disappointed idealist who saw nothing ahead for man but an apocalyptic cataclysm? Both these interpretations have been maintained and both today are being abandoned by careful study. Gautama the Buddha is seen to have taught a lofty Protestantism—the right of the soul, the essential need of the soul, to seek its source and salvation within; leaving aside rituals and sacrifices, theories and speculations. Jesus the Christ taught the same eternal gospel, the Kingdom is within you. They start from different ends of the one great bridge that links God and man, but each completes the span and confirms the other's route: for it is the same route whether traversed from the one end or from the other. We may perhaps put in a phrase the contrast and confirmation each teaching gives to the other. Buddha raised Immanence to Transcendence: "The Self, the abiding Presence in the heart, is the Lord of the self, of the individual consciousness." That was simply to put in the simplest language the great keystone phrase of the Upanishads—those primal scriptures of our race—"He that dwells in the heart is also he who dwells in the sun, who transcends the universe." Christ brought down Transcendence to Immanence. "I and my Father are one: I in you and you in me."

Now let us look at these initial words about sorrow. Christ says, "Blessed are they that mourn for they shall be comforted." Buddha too begins his teaching with, "I show you sorrow and the ending of sorrow." But the Beatitudes have already let us some way into the secret. We are being emptied that we may be filled. The first Beatitude is a whole category in itself. That was the primary stage of that growth, of that psychic evolution called the Mystic way. That primary stage is Purgation. After that we enter a second series of developmental levels. This series which we are now entering is called that of the Proficients. What does this Proficiency mean? It is the same as being adept and an adept is one, the word's origin shows, who has attained insight. He has risen to the height where he can make the Great Diagnosis. He sees through appearances. He sees the visible world as a profoundly significant symptom, profoundly disquieting if nothing is done about it or if it is misread. He sees that the condition is far graver than it appears to a superficial glance. So this sad searching look is the first step that the cleared mind must take. It must face up to the situation that discloses itself when the mists of self-illusion are dissipated. Then after diagnosis comes the treatment. The proficient passes from mourning —from facing frankly the actual sorriness of his and his fellows' state—on to treatment, to being trained in an athletic and dynamic acceptance. Then—final term of proficiency—final achievement of the new life, vitality and health, there arises in him a new appetite, a new keen hunger, the creative desire to grow.

This sorrow is no comprehensive, fundamental, paralyzing pessimism. It does not say, "I tell you

life is a cruel fraud for all, and consciousness is for
every sentient creature, a continuous agony or a
series of clever reliefs and cunning lures so as to
make its suffering more acute." True, both these
messages have been so interpreted, and so the gospel
of deliverance, dynamic compassion and enlightenment has been construed as simply a suicide's coun-
sel dressed in sanctimonious parlance; likewise the
gospel of a loving Father and a world in which
Heaven is always present, as long as self is absent,
was made to read as the dealings of a pitiless judge
with an earth, fallen, poisoned and cursed and with
a race, bitter, hating and hated by its creator. No,
what both these sublime utterances of the spirit
say to, and are answered by, the spirit in our hearts
is something quite different. They say, "I show you
sorrow and I come not to the healthy but to the
sick, not because the Spirit rejects, far less sneers at
all who are happy, healthy, innocent." Christ says
there are the whole, the healthy, the simply straight-
forwardly sane, the unreflectively happy, the innocent, who, as children see, see the intense moment
shining in its timelessness, unshadowed by past
regret or future apprehension. But for most of us
that singleness of vision has been lost. How and
why it first slipped away neither Christ nor Buddha
will tell. "Offenses must needs come," is the basis
and datum line drawn by Christ along that frontier
of mystery, the origin of evil, the beginning and
cause of sorrow. Buddha points out that such ques-
tionings can only delay men caught in sin and
misery from escaping. He asks, would you waste the

precious seconds questioning the doctor about his skin color or other irrelevancies while he was waiting to remove a poisoned arrow from your side? Once the wound is clean and the poison out of the system you will have time, detachment and competence to deal with abstract questions. Once delivered you will be enlightened and once enlightened you will understand what before must be incomprehensible.

So there is authentic happiness in the world, for there is much life that has yet to be egoistic and self-centered, self-conscious. We ourselves may at moments, as Wordsworth said, have "Intimations of Immortality," and even in late life when men find nothing fresh to delight in and no spontaneity springing up within them, for

> "Custom lies upon them with a weight
> Heavy as frost and deep almost as life"

even then, though ever more rarely and faintly,

> "In a season of calm weather
> Though inland far we be
> Our souls have sight of that immortal sea which brought
> us hither."

There is an animal immortality, a clear, untroubled joy which is always gleaming where the river of life breaks out from its source and before those waters have become muddied by time. The light of the Eternal Life shines through all unstudied unself-conscious beings, "For is not He all save that which is doomed to say I am I?"

But having allowed that, having rejoiced in it, we must, with equal clarity, equal honesty allow two further things about that happiness. The first thing is that it is not for us. The fact that we are self-conscious and cannot stop being self-conscious by any effort of the will—rather aggravating it—debars us from returning to that Eden. The second thing is even more baffling. It is the question whether—let alone we could ever get back there—whether the Eden we look at and long for is there, as we think we see it. Not only can we ourselves never re-enter that world of unreflective happiness—we cannot really understand it. No lesson of natural history has been more necessary and more startling to us than this: "Do not put yourself in the other's place if that other is a wild animal." Your whole sense of increasing worth in life is based on increasing fore-sight—consciousness extended beyond the immediate. Its entire peace of mind is based on having no foresight. It is immortal and has the happiness of the immortal just as long and just because it has no time sense, no past and no future. We would give animals protection, make the individual animal last to old age, render it, if we might, cautious, circum-spect, able to "look before and after," and so to "sigh for what is not." As far as we teach them our consciousness and strive to give them our security we must awake in them—as indeed it would seem we often do with some of our pets—a sense of anxiety, a sense of Time. We are removing their natural protection, their blessed ignorance, their power of instantaneity, letting the penumbra of time infringe on the bright flash of their eternity. We who are creatures of anxiety, always trying to fight time with time, in attempting to give them our febrile defenses, we are destroying their own utterly different defense against disaster, as, by wrapping up our bodies we lose the body's natural resistance-reaction to cold. No doubt (and there is not a little evidence for this) a saint, one who had emerged at the other end into the light of eternity, can get into touch with beasts, understand and love their nature without disturbing it and receive their love and trust, for he does not disturb their ignorance of time. He does not attempt to make them time-conscious, because he is, himself, no longer time-conscious. But we cannot. All we can say is that there is a happiness behind us, as well as in front of us. There is this hinter-happiness but there is this strange doom attached to it that it must never know that it is happy, it must never say, "I am blessed." Let it think for one moment, let it reflect and, like a plane stopping dead in full flight, it must fall headlong.

Here lies the profoundest of Life's mysteries—the mystery of Time. Simple Pessimism, "All life is wretched, overshadowed by fear." Simple Optimism, "All life is happy, provided it does not chill its blood with thinking." Neither of these conclusions covers the facts. There is an animal immortality and in that, no doubt, a profound sense of completeness. But that state begins to be overclouded the moment there is any reflection upon it, indeed any awareness of it. We can then hardly describe any living creature as wholly happy, for entire happiness could only belong to the completely unaware, to the lifeless. Life, consciousness which is Life's accompaniment, is of its nature a being separate; a knowing that one is oneself and not all; a power to compare and so to realize that everything is passing. At first, no doubt, this is very dim; but it is there from the beginning, misting the bright mirror. And of necessity it must spread and darken. To know clearly that living is good is to know at the same instant that life is evil also. The Tree of the Knowledge of Good is also the Tree of the Knowledge of Evil.

This is the truth which truthful natural history will no longer let us gloze. We have sentimentalized over Nature. First it was all sweet and innocent, and all we needed to be happy was to take off our clothes, discard our taboos and obey impulse. That soon showed itself to be nonsense. Then we rushed to the other extreme, shuddering at "Nature red in tooth and claw with ravine shrieking at our creed." Animals may have happiness but it is not ours because their consciousness is not ours. Life, like Wisdom, is probably "justified of all her children"; life is worth while to each but not in terms which we can understand. We now can see therefore that when, in our sentimentalism, we would make a wild creature comfortable, as we feel and conceive comfort, we destroy what they have, the immediate happiness of their health and appetites, in the vain attempt to give them, what we long for but ourselves never attain, security. We feed the bear and not having to find their food they become ailing: we remove the mountain lion and the deer become diseased. We castrate the domestic cat to relieve it of its passions but its lime secretion is thereby often upset and so instead of exciting wounds it has the cold aching misery of stone. What is our sentiment doing? It is trying to stop time. We must not, we cannot arrest the animal, whether the wild animal or the animal in ourselves. It must run through its cycle and its immortality is not in individual longevity but in the cycle of the race. When it has grown and begotten and reared healthy begetters, the light of life is already shining in the next generation. Aristotle's famous dictum, "After coitus all animals are sad," is still anthropomorphic. It should run, "After coitus all animals are more than half anaesthetized, more than half dead and done with." The animal is ageless not because it can delay oncoming death but, on the contrary, because the life within it discards the body as soon as Death begins to find purchase on that husk. The life within it plunges into Death as a dust-caked and blinded runner plunges into a stream crossing his path, sluices off his incrustation and, freshly lithe again, springs once more on his way. Animal life is happy precisely because the vast majority alive must always be those at the height of their physical fitness. Any beginning to ail or age is quickly killed off.

But what about children? Surely they are happy? Yes, but under the same law, that they must not dwell in their happiness; as Wordsworth says, they must be "blindly with their happiness at strife." If we are only animals then we *should be* too old at forty. It is then time for the children whom we healthily begot in our prime, themselves to be raising their brood, themselves to be the elders; and we must be discarded as the flower discards the sheath, and the fruit, the flower. Life can begin at forty but it must be a real beginning, a new birth, a second growth. It is not a continuation of animal life, through rejuvenation or auto-suggestion, but the death of the old life and the beginning of the life eternal. Indeed we have seen in the last twenty years that in the dictatorial countries where the evolution of consciousness, the growth of the soul is denied, where fit animal living and the life of the race and the state is the one permitted end, in such states, a man is an encumbrance, a problem, an anomaly when he is an elderly animal. That must be so. If in animal life only, in a Utopia of fine physicalness, we alone have hope, then you must prune out old age as drastically as we prune old wood out of a fruit tree, or eugenists would prune out congenital idiocy. But there is no stopping this knife once it has begun to lop. We have to shear down till we find a creature so animal that it can never reflect, always act, always lust. If in establishing a life of animal happiness we alone have hope we are indeed of all animals the most miserable.

To every human being there must therefore come, soon or late, a time when the child brightness is lost. True, in times of quiet, as has been said, an echo, a recollection of that happiness will return but only as an echo. Then it fades and returns no more. Then a man knows despair—despair which lures the more hopeful to suicide. The rest just die a lingering death from mortification of the soul. Such sorrow is a turning point; that sadness is not blessed in itself for in itself it does not lead to comfort. It is, if it stays at that level, only that self-pity which is pride—always an ugly thing even when alive—in an advanced state of decomposition. But if poverty of spirit has been granted then the pity will not stop at self-pity. True, if left to itself, it looks as though life, as it now is, very seldom can achieve a whole age of innocency from youth to death. Most have a gleam at sunrise and from thence on the day clouds and lowers to its close. That is the normal natural course for that unnatural animal man.

And therefore it is precisely at this point that Salvation and its Good News enter. Here we see the inexhaustible creativeness of the love of God. The subconscious drive, the unquestioning, unreflective openness of life was failing; whether slowly or by some sudden break, whether by a sudden fall, a single decisive wrong choice or by a slow and growing error we cannot say. The goal, if things were left to themselves, must be tragedy, squalor, collapse, futility, ruin. Then the free creativeness freely intervenes. That is the doctrine of the incarnation. We shall find this fact coming back again later. Here we can say, the very breakdown and discord is made by the Eternal Creativeness to be able to be resolved into a higher harmony. That is why Augustine, and many other saints who sank to rise, can cry, O Felix Culpa, fortunate fault whereby by grace a richer condition is permitted than ever could have belonged to unreflective, unself-conscious innocency. Poverty of spirit being given a man, he can suddenly see himself, see that all his pain, all pain comes from that strangulation of consciousness which we call our ego, our personality. Then, though his sorrow remains, it suddenly changes its nature, its temperature. That deadly inflowing tide of freezing despair is reversed and becomes another outflowing current of warm compassion. "The tears in things" which Virgil felt to be the very essence of life, are still here but they are no longer of heartbroken sorrow but of relief. They flow from the sudden sense of kinship with all the lonely, the sundered, the lost. They are painful but it is the pain of a returning circulation. The pain is welcomed because it is surety of recovery. It is pledge of our eternal and infinite life through God in all our fellows, in all life; through our fellows and through all life in God. So this mourning is not to lead us on to a high lonely Stoical despair. It brings us round in a spiral to a restoration of innocency. We become like children but children who can remember and can foresee, adults who dare remember and dare foresee.

Does this seem a glib escape out of the problem of suffering? Is this argument no more than an emulsion made by blending a few ancient orthodox terms with a thought or two from modern natural history? Such it may seem to some, even of those who trouble to read these lines. May then this thought such as it is, be taken a step further. Granted that sorrow always seems to come with self-consciousness, that, in Paul's phrase, "until there was the Law"—the knowledge of a principle which required to be observed—"there was no sin," is then sorrow, is then sin, inescapable? We must first ask, is self-consciousness itself a mistake, an error, a sin? That can hardly be so, for if it were, then all life has followed a mistaken course. That conclusion has been held by some—by some Buddhists, yes, and by some Christians. Indeed the strict doctrine of Original Sin seems to necessitate such a conclusion. Indeed so authoritative a Doctor of the Western Church, St. Gregory the Great, theologian and pope, taught[1] with consistency that reproduction was regrettable for it involved more souls in the Original Sin and in the high risk of everlasting damnation. But most devout thinkers of every spiritual church, East or West, have felt that the conclusion cannot be as simple as that. Self-consciousness in itself is not sin. It is a state in which sin can be committed, as it could not be before. Therefore, and this is the interesting conclusion, it would be possible for man to attain self-consciousness without sin. That conclusion is so interesting, so vital, because, instead of bringing our thought up against a blank wall, it leads on a step, a very important step. What, in the simplest psychological language, has happened to us? Each of us seems to recapitulate in our individ-

[1] See his Sermon at the Marriage of Two Nobles.

ual selves the psychological story of our race. Briefly it is this: We begin by being happy without knowing it; then it dawns on us that we are happy. There is no harm in that. The slip comes not here but at the next step. Finding we are happy we try and hold fast and fixed to this happiness, this precise state; we fear to go on, we refuse to be weaned and to sample further fare. We try even more violently to ward off all intrusion and possible trespass on our little lit field of delight and, as we turn to attack intruders, the happiness is gone. Now that line of life, that curve of growth so seen, has a hope for us. For it shows three things: Firstly, that it is not self-consciousness which is the mistake. Secondly, that the mistake is something which we make and do, freely; because it is done after we became aware of being happy, it is an act of will, of deliberate refusal. And thirdly, that this mistake is made and done not because of awareness, of self-consciousness, but, on the contrary, through our not being sufficiently aware, sufficiently self-conscious. We see then that the mistake is not to be remedied by an attempted retreat into unself-consciousness. Evolution is irreversible: it is impossible for us to go back. If it were possible it would only prove that the whole process of life was a futile mistake. All life has led to consciousness.

We must go on further. But what if we are hopelessly bogged? Here comes in the further aspect of hope. If failure has been due, not to the life process itself, but to some mistaken choice, some act of will made by the creature when it was brought to the point where it could choose its way up or down, there could be a type, a strain, a line of creatures which always accepted, always felt and answered the urge to advance and embrace and never yielded to the temptation to arrest, retreat, reject. At the level of life's beginnings such an urge would—say in the primitive form of protoplasm—be a constant seeking and expanding rather than shrinking, withdrawing, secreting. Instead of shell and armor, seal, shutter and anchor, it would be free, moving, lithe, agile, aware.[2] As, in consequence of this open striving, intenser consciousness shone in it, the creature would experience and manifest constantly growing wonder, interest and sympathy. So, up the whole ladder of life, the tree of evolution, a consistent acceptance would guide its life, until, when self-conscious manhood was attained, there would be disclosed a being born wholly free of those sudden reflexes of retreat, those inherited spasms of doubt and denial. Such a being, because he had never diverged from the straight path of life, could rise indefinitely and, what is more, by the trueness, undeviatingness, of his ascent, by, not only his demonstration that this is the way of life (all else leads to death), but also by the fact that this his way of life *means* the embracing of others, he could salvage us.

Yet, because his power is co-operative power, because it works by appeal and not by coercion, it operates first by inspiration, by awaking in us the

[2] It is a significant fact that many of the shelled creatures seem to have formed this hard husk owing to the fact that the sessile life into which they sank did not permit their organism to rid itself of its superfluous lime.

wish to have such power of acceptance. Then, once we have the wish, we find that we are gathered back into this dynamic, ever-expanding unity, in which these leaders live.

So, if we are to accept the aid of those saviors who have saved themselves "to eternal life" by never saving themselves here and now, we too must partake of their divine lack of limit, circumspection and liability. But we cannot do that, it is too much to ask of us as an act of blind faith. Verbal assent only makes the reflexes deny the more stubbornly. "Acceptance" is a popular word today. "Just accept life" has become the great slogan rising from a concordat between the churches whose "social gospel" has just failed and a psychiatry which is just hoping to succeed—perhaps in curing the patients, probably in cornering the practice. But however often I say the blessed word "accept," how shall I make my deep self really do so? "Just open your eye!" urges the helpful friend when we have a sharp cinder in it, while he dabs with his handkerchief at our shrinking lid. He is right we know, but open up we cannot. Some one must speak to us, must speak for us, so that our shrinking silly reflex, powerful echo of our past denials and refusals, may stop spoiling the salvage—so that our inherited stupidity and suspicion may listen, obey, trust. The only persons who can speak to us and bid us come forth are those who themselves have always accepted all and so can accept for us. The Sons, they can say yes for us in our name, and in so far as we accept in their name.

This is an immense mystery, always capable of

being further misunderstood the further it is illustrated. Yet the above words may perhaps stand, for they may speak, not as instruction, but as confirmation to some other seeker. What can be said, with less fear of "darkening knowledge with words," is that today we can hope to understand in modern terminology why it is that the Sons can so accept. We can see what a comprehensive meaning they and they alone can show to reside in life by their taking what seem to us impossible risks and by their deliberate choice of what seems to us the path not of sensible security and comfort but of sorrow. Our being ignorant of this fact, that there are such Sons, is the cause of our mistaken attitude toward sorrow. Not knowing that there can be a human type which is free because it has not committed the Original Sin of retreat into the self, we are of necessity ignorant of that truth's corollary. The Sons show us three things: that theirs has been the path of Evolution; that Evolution continues in them now; and that following them we can return to and continue our Evolution. We have feared sorrow and shrunk from discomfort because we took for granted that Evolution must be over, there could be no further development ahead for us. Change is always uncomfortable, distressing, dis-easing. If any change must be for the worse (for we, being at the top, the only possible alteration must be downward), naturally pain could only be taken as a symptom of oncoming decay and collapse. But if we are still to grow then pain can be growing pain.

That, in a phrase, is the comfort, the comforting

which makes the mourning blessed. By poverty of spirit, by forsaking the self and its false wish to attain an isolated happiness and (that failing) an isolated despair, our natural inevitable sorrow and self-pity was released from its vicious circling round the self, and, so sent out, it melts, like an equatorial current the ice-locked shores of other lands. Of course that is somewhat different a definition of comfort than that much used, much lounged-in word now carries. Few words have so degenerated under materialism. When we reflect that the Third Person of the Trinity is specifically named the Comforter we can gauge the enormity of the fall which such a word has suffered in its significance. That the tremendous aspect of Godhead, the creative Thought which manifested the whole visible creation out of the void, that incessant unwearied Inspiration which stirs and sustains the whole of life to express itself, that power of Insight whereby consciousness can clear until it understands its source and attains union with its original Being and Goal, that such a mystery of Living Power should now be named by the word Comforter is perhaps the strangest freak of language. Yet it is not a freak but a symptom. Comfort—the word still shows its great origin in its grammatical structure—is not ease, least of all physical ease and well-padded lassitude. It is, at the least, athletic strength and resiliency. It is, in its full sense, that inspiration which speaks in the heart as that firm assurance which is courage, and in the head as that faith which is not credulity but the wise and clear choice of the nobler hypothesis.

We have suffered from a shallow optimism. Because we read of the saints, the perfecti, the souls united with God making no longer any struggle, we thought the spiritual life throughout was carried on effortlessly. There is one extenuating circumstance to excuse such silliness. In the West there can be no doubt there was often a serious confusion made between asceticism, intelligent athletic effort, stern but skilled discipline, and mortification, the torture of the body. Those Egyptian desert Fathers who influenced so heavily Christian mysticism were foolishly fond of saying that a sick body was the best base for a healthy soul. Hence when mortification was abandoned as unwise it was thought that the only alternative was to make no effort. Because a clumsily performed Caesarean operation is a highly dangerous, indeed generally a fatal obstetric practice, that does not mean that birth is without labor and that delivery is possible without skilled help and acute effort. Mourning is necessary because we have to die to much in which we assumed our happiness to live. The animal which is about to metamorphize, retires from its former life and goes through a death—a death of distinct risk and a birth of great labor and peril. Even the snake seems to sicken as it casts its skin, the birds become dumb and listless while they moult. We have to draw in ourselves, to abandon all those other contacts and supports which helped to make life pleasant and gave it purpose. We have to throw ourselves wholly into the deep of Being, a blind sinking. No, that cannot be pleasant or easy. But unless we do so we shall never gain the recreative Comfort. There is a time when we have definitely to leave hold of the appearance, that we may sound the Reality; to abandon our grip on all our surface supports that we may directly experience that underneath are the Everlasting Arms.

If we really can give up all hope in man—not in violent despair but quietly and rationally because we know that all our hope can be, must be, and shall be in God alone, then, having no hope any longer in ourselves and humanity, the Divine Comforter is nigh even at the door. We have to cease to have any pleasure in anything but God, and so deeply blinding may those pleasures have been that when we have given them up we may not be able to find Him. That is often due to the fact that we look for Him in the shape and form of those pleasures—as a kindly friend, an indulgent Father, a Creator who creates toys for his children at their every whim. We have to stand in the dark till our eyes can see, until our hearts cease their greedy wish for any comfort save that He Is. When we learn that, then we cease to care so much whether we are ourselves comforted. We begin to feel a universal compassion and suddenly in this is His coming, His presence.

This, then, it would seem, is the reason why the mourners, who have won the right to a creative compassion, a wise sorrow which is without heartbreak, are blessed because they are so comforted.

They see of the travail of the soul and are satisfied because they see the redemptive process at work, that redemptive process which more than restores the simple innocency of an unaware creation, of a life which may be happy but only if it never understands and only if it shuns those, the sick and the despairing, who have eaten of the Fruit of the Tree of the Knowledge of Good and Evil. These blessed sad do more: they do not merely see, they find themselves, thawed out by their compassion, taking actual part in the redemptive work by realizing and living in the realization of their fellowship with all who are also in the agony of deliverance from the self. With that comfort and compassion, as an alternating current flowing through them, the sense of kinship being matched by the sense of power, the knowledge of unity with man leading back to the inspiring revelation of the union with God, the soul is ready to mount another rung of the ladder, the third— that third Blessedness which is to be for the meek and which is to give them, as the outlook from that their station, the inheritance of the earth.

# IV.

## PROFICIENCY—ii

### *The Way of Training*

✜✜✜✜✜✜✜✜✜✜✜✜✜✜✜✜✜✜✜✜✜✜✜✜✜✜✜✜✜✜✜✜✜✜✜✜✜✜✜✜

*"Blessed are the meek for they shall inherit the earth."*

We are, it is clear when we look at this the third title, still in that range and level of spiritual thought where paradox must still rule. We are still so unaccustomed to spiritual truths that they must sound, must be put to us in terms which seem contradiction. The poor-spirited are in the Kingdom as its natural inevitable owners. The mourners are to be congratulated for it is they and not the happy and prosperous who have coming to them the fundamental and final satisfaction of that ceaselessly upholding and upspringing strength which is right comfort. And now a third time, it is again just those whom common sense believes to be out of the running, out of luck, unworthy of anything but, at best, a superficial patronizing pity, it is a class whom the world rejects, which is picked for commendation and reward. And when we look at the reward and reason we are more surprised than even at the two earlier resultants. After all, the Kingdom of Heaven is God's, and quite mysteriously un-

known to most of us and to all men who pride themselves on being practical; and the comforting of
mourners may well be a mysterious dispensation of
that supremely mysterious Being the Comforter.
But though "the heaven is the Lord's, the earth hath
He given to the children of men," and certainly they
have shown no hesitation in handling it as they
have seen fit, until, whatever it is, it can hardly be
said to be a fit place for anyone meek, let alone as
a place which such characters are to rule.

Yet as the other paradoxes yield their divine sense
under study, let us first see what the phrase means
in itself. Who are the meek and (this will pretty
certainly throw some light on who they are) why
is it so divinely suitable that they should inherit the
earth? We have seen that the other two earlier
states could be understood by the condition and
place to which they lead those who are in them.
There is certainly no random raining of rewards in
the Beatitudes, as buns are pelted at bears. Each
reward is, as is always with God's grants, an inevitable result, for He is all Love and all Law, His
acts are both free grace and sure consequence. Each
reward, too, is, we have seen, dependent on the
reward acquired before. Here then we shall see that
the steady outpouring, the redemptive process, is,
at the third level, extended. The process began, at
the first level, where all recreative processes must
begin, in the soul of man. That, therefore, is a
stage complete in itself. That first rung covers a
whole epoch of man's spiritual evolution. It in-
cludes, we have seen, the entire first third of the

ascent to God, the epoch of Purgation. Then, on rung two the process of Purgation is sufficiently complete, the obstructions sufficiently reduced. So we enter on the stage of Proficiency. The redemptive process has risen high enough in the heart, for the power now begins to flow out and to act on other souls drawing them, in turn, onto the first level of deliverance from their egos. And now in stage three that power is ready to become manifest in and to the world at large. The seed in the soul, on first break-ing its husk, puts down its root, then begins to thrust up its shoot. Finally, in the third stage of its growth, it first becomes visible above earth, to the world. But, before we go on with our study of this the third stage's linked relationship with the other six rungs and levels, we must examine as closely as we can the clause itself.

The meek, the least likely of all the seven types, are to inherit the least likely of stations. The poor in spirit, now that we see that they are for all intents and purposes invisible, might slip in and, a sort of spiritual fifth column or Trojan horse, by sheer skill in concealment, worm themselves by back stairs, if not into office at least to where they might lurk behind some big executive chair. The mourn-ers, if they are really sympathetic characters, men and women who are really sorry for others, might be flung some fragment of the spoils of office; for the powerful are often longing to be pitied and will pay well to have the services of those who can do it convincingly. They want an unambitious intimate on whose shoulder they can weep with self-pity when they have just liquidated an ungrateful colleague. The merciful, as they, evidently, are powerful enough to be able to spare an enemy, they, too, might get a slice of worldly power in exchange. The children of God, yes, they also are more likely, for, after all, God does rule and God only knows what He might do. Of course those who are so hungry over righteousness and those who only want to see God are out of the running, but even they are not such positively improbable candidates for ownership of the earth as the meek. Certainly that phrase does bring us up with something of a shock. Is this, after all, mere paradox, just putting everything on its head because in this mad world things may well make some sort of better sense than they do now, standing as they are?

Certainly though generosity and sympathy are not aggressive qualities and do not seem to get you far in the world as it is, yet they are not provocative qualities. Meekness is. Aesop's wolf was not speaking barefaced cynicism when he said that the lamb was provocative.

Biology is showing that there is a deep terrible partnership between the ruminants and the carnivores. As the ungulates, the hoofed animals let their hand become mutilated into a single monstrous calloused finger, a pole with which to jump from one grazing to another, the unguiculates, the clawed animals let their hand (till then not so mutilated as the ruminants) turn on this tempting flesh and their paws became taloned and their teeth became fanged. So the carnivore has been degraded into a parasite, an automatized slayer and we despise and fear the creeping killer. But this is only half of the full picture. The carnivore could not exist were it not that first the ruminants existed: that is one side of the proposition. But the converse is equally true, though less spectacular: the ruminants have, by their vital degeneracy, which led to their deforming specialization, so diminished their inborn power to respond to life that in their bodies the vital energy is now so sluggish that, as already noted, if they are not continually spurred on by the fear and fact of pursuit, their vitality fails and the herds and flocks are devastated far more by disease than by slaughter. The beasts of fodder and the beasts of prey now make together a mysterious balance. Both stocks refused to find a balance of life in its own stock and so if they are to survive at all they must be, as it were, propped against one another. We can now see that not only are the weaklings of the herd and flock picked off but also that those who get away are roused by their fear and anger to a higher vitality. Under this "chivying" not only do the feeble fall out, but the strong become stronger until they can hit back at their scourge—when it begins to fail. They become once more slack. The scourge again grows, and so the cycle continues.

These painful facts apply also to us. The degenerate notion of comfort made a new word come into our language, a new evil into our consciousness. That is Boredom; a word not found in Dr. Johnson's dictionary and first experienced (in the Modern Age) in that world of arrested energy and wit, the Court of Louis XIV. Nearly all men are quickly staled by security. Leisure, which once meant the time which a man could have for his private interests, now means having nothing to do—vacuity. Such leisure is a negative pain which grows in intensity, a spreading ache in the mind akin to hunger. Risk and danger banish that. Hence we have sport and gambling as the chief interest of most people who have arrived at leisure, for these things give a vicarious excitement. Living is no longer enough in itself. Soon these pretense perils and artificial risks are not enough. We must have the real thing. There is, short of Ecstasy—the Ecstasy of creativeness, of love, of divine self-loss—no pleasure equal to that felt in the escape from deadly fear. If you cannot give a man ecstasy sooner or later he will take to self-torture and challenge others to torture.

It is this terrible cycle of interdependence between man and man, beast and beast, which we have overlooked. We saw only one side. The truth is that we are all tied up in "the bundle of Life" far more closely than we could think. If we will not love our fellow man we shall not escape kinship with him. Love him or hate him, these are the only alternatives offered us: draw him out to co-operate with us or provoke him to compete with us. By our deep common nature we may not be indifferent to him. Man can only find his full capacity of expression and so his full happiness with man. We must realize then that there is always present a subtle provocation of which the "assaultee" is not innocent. The actual outburst was only a spark which fired the imperceptibly accumulated charge.

It has been pointed out that, if we would understand murder, we must recognize that, beside the murderer there is another factor, indeed another actor in the crime—that is the "murderee." The Law stops at the immediate cause, but justice must trace the disordered balance farther back, if the reason for violence is to be understood. Nor are we at the bottom of the mystery when we have found that most murders are done by men against women, and those women have moved men emotionally. The nagging wife, the provocative sweetheart may, we all know, make their murder fifty per cent suicide. But apart from these, violence, even then, is not without defense in saying it was provoked. Fear, cravenness, the meekness which is always telling everyone it meets that he is the kind of man who beats up strangers without cause, and that he really must let this poor lamb pass for once, wolf though he is, that attitude is irritating to those who till then were feeling neither an impulse to bully nor to cringe. The ape-like animal in everyone is not a beast but it is easily upset, made disquieted, resentful and angry by being treated as though it were an ill-conditioned, evil-tempered cur. Every human contact and meeting is a mysterious sacramental thing. Whether we will or no, we have to approach our fellow man every time we meet with an anxiety-hope. The unspoken unconscious question in our minds has first to be: Will he recognize we are one—not effusively—that is simply the surface mind trying to deny the deep mind's refusal—but by taking for granted we shall get on, that we shall like each other, entertain each other because we both are human; or will he be defensive, treating me as someone who would take what he would not give and incapable of giving anything that he would welcome? That contact or that break is made without words; is made, irrevocable generally, long before words can be spoken, sometimes when still out of earshot. These facts have been proved with animals. We cannot argue with them, prove our good intentions, point out to them why they should not bite us. Our attitude, our unspoken feeling-tone settles all that in advance.

In short fear is the converse, the cause, the match which fired the mine of anger. Fear indeed is negative anger, the negative pole to which must rush the positive charge of rage. We do insult a man by fearing him: we dislike him and thrust him from our communion.

And that precisely is what meekness is nearly always doing—or at least what we call meekness. Can it be such—can it be people so inclined to shun, subconsciously suspect and secede from their fellow men—can these inherit this teeming earth? There certainly is cause for further inquiry here and that inquiry is certainly repaid. What is the precise meaning of this keyword meek? We shall find there is an interesting mystery here if we open a French New Testament, for there this Beatitude wears a different dress, certainly less dowdy, more gallant, more French. This third Blessing runs—"Blessed are the Debonair." That is a startling, gay contrast. Instead of the motto being, "Please don't kick me," we find, "Please let me know if there is anything I can do for you." The man with good airs and pleasant graces, in short the gentleman, has taken the place of the defensive, down-at-heels who hopes you won't notice him or call upon him. The man who knows how to behave, who always has the easy gracious initiative because he always holds to his own standards however others may forget themselves, because he always conducts himself as though the other man must *au fond* be a gentleman, even if momentarily flustered and needing his temporary embarrassment to be covered, that is the Debonair and that the French translators of the Gospel Greek, picked as the word to render what our translators rendered meek. We can't help feeling that it must be too French, too hopeful, too much due to an amiable Gallic courtesy-wish to make the Gospel ideal appear after all no more and no less than a French gentleman, *le beau idéal*. Yet there must have been some ground for this amazing rendering.

Let us turn then to the Greek itself—not the word Jesus spoke but at least a language bilingually familiar to his biographers, and not impossibly to himself. What is the Greek testament word which we have now rendered as "meek"? It is *praos*[1] (πραος). For what did Greeks use it? They used it for wild animals which had been tamed, trained, for wild horses which had been made able to work with men. There is then in this definition, nothing

[1] See Appendix for more detailed textual treatment.

[63]

weak or spiritless but rather the description of an energy which, instead of exploding, is now channeled and directed. The tamed are not the tame, people who are born empty and have no inner force to master, no vitality to be taught control. The trained are those whose powerful impulses have been put into understanding service. When we have dug out that meaning from the heart of this word then we see the high sense of using it in this Beatitude. We can realize why such a type would naturally, inevitably be the sort which would inherit the earth. The trained always have won against the untrained. What is more, the most daring individual courage and impulsive dash have again and again crumpled before men carefully conditioned. Further, it has been shown that by careful training the most unpromising material can be made more reliable than the best native attack. We can also see why this type comes where it does on the ladder of Perfection. First man is emptied of himself; then he is given both a sense of Life's tragedy, that much is gravely wrong, and also the hope that it can and will be put right and restored. Therefore now man has to be told about his actual part in this restorative task in the actual world.

Now that we see this meekness is what a medieval mystic calls "a work of meeking," we may inquire about how it is done. What sort of training is this beatific training? It is not ordinary training. Ordinary training wins against the untrained. But today, the world is full of trained men, destroying others similarly trained, men just as highly disciplined and unquestioningly devoted. What we are watching today is the tragedy of inapt force reducing civilization to anarchy. We are seeing high courage and intense skill canceling out an equal courage and skill. In a world, where our God-given power of order and intelligence has only begun the work of banishing ignorance, lethargy, disease, we see the forces of intelligence, order, discipline and fitness turning on each other. Ignorance, lethargy and disease return again, retake the offensive and the battle of united humanity; for united humanity, by united humanity, is lost.

No one suspected this could befall such as we. Barbarians might arise, gather and sweep in from beyond the bounds of civilization. Pestilences might spread and devastate. But the reservoirs of true barbarism, where war is endemic and fighting the normal exercise of simple, untaught kinesthetic tribes, these areas were becoming ordered, this boisterous energy canalised. The pestilences, too, seemed hemmed, weakened, controlled. And then it was that the very people whose efficient energies led such triumphs of ordered intelligence, turned from mankind's common foes onto themselves. This is not a return to disorder, anarchy, barbarism, savagery. This is ordered intelligence confounded by itself. There is no end to this but the destruction of all order and understanding, discipline and devotion—unless there can be found a still higher training yielding a yet higher, apter power. The powers as they are now opposed are equally matched. For on neither side (each vowed to destroy the other) is there a decisive superiority in physical skill or disciplined devotion. Neither side knows of any method or means, of any force, radically different from and superior to the other's. They must both attempt to win victory with weapons which are inept and which grow increasingly inept, for these weapons are weapons of indirect action, clumsy pressure. They madden rather than persuade, awake desperation rather than concession, devastate rather than secure.

It is then painfully clear that our position is one of ghastly paradox. The more intelligent we are, the more insane and brutal is our action. The more disciplined and devoted, the more we spread chaos and anarchy. The more ordered, the faster we bring on civilization's collapse. Order may be Heaven's first law; we certainly cannot, dare not stop at it. And the reason for this horrible confusion is equally clear. We stopped short with an inadequate training. We thought we knew enough both as to our powers and our duty, both as to what kind of force was needed to make the world a noble design for living and what standard of training was required to handle that force wisely and well. We imagined that all we needed were the obvious animal virtues of courage and devotion to one's neighbor, the love of one's friend and the wary respect of one's enemy, and the secondary virtues of temperance, accuracy, prudence and vigilance. The unlimited devotion expressed by the adoration of God, the unlimited faith sprung, and alone to be sprung, from the faith in God, that faith, which knows Him to be so real that only by complete love and understanding may He or any of His children be served—that we considered unnecessary, otiose, an extravagant idealism. It was not. It was as necessary though as unnoticed as vitamins in food or oxygen in air. For truth is more than accuracy; righteousness more than efficiency; love more than a liking for one's neighbor. The trained, as we have the world full of them today, will never inherit the earth. Their broken bones and flesh will feed its soil, which the insects, safely denied our deadly powers, will inhabit. Our species might hang on, one of the larger apes but inefficient at that:

> Despised by the chimpanzees
> Because we leap so clumsily and bruise so badly
> When we tumble from the trees.

Yet training is not a mistake. Lethargy is lower than energy. We must go through the lower power, understanding, devotion and discipline, on to the higher.

And the way is marked: the process is divided for us into two stages—indeed perhaps we may say into three. For first we have to be caught. As Paul says—he who heard a voice saying, "Why do *you* persecute me? It is hard to kick against the barbed wire."—The love of God constrains us, lassoes us. We find ourselves corralled. Then we are trained, conditioned to work obediently, in blinkers if need be, beside the Other who yokes himself with us. We are at laborer level, at field-beast service. But there is a third stage above being trained—that is being tamed. We are brought into the house; we become companions of the Master. This is not imagery; it is exactitude. This is the path and process whereby wild animals are brought into full touch with man. The height of taming is complete domestication. And we must note, this final training is quite beyond, and has in it quite a different quality from the first training. It is the new turn of the spiral, when the freedom, which the animal had as a wild animal, is given back to it. But this release is given back because something else, quite another freedom, a fundamental liberty which the wild had lost, is now restored. The wild beast, cat or dog, horse or gazelle, when wild is not free at all, in this full sense. It is gyved and collared by its specialized reactions, those specializations which, as we have seen, have made the carnivores parasitic for their food on the ruminants and (just as much) the ruminants dependent for their health on the carnivores.

This further story of what can only be called psycho-biological redemption, has been worked out, for example, in the classic study "The Dog as the Foetalization of the Wolf." The wolf is a highly specialized creature and so, of necessity, a beast with very narrowed reactions. Physique and psyche —skull-shape and no brain; jaw and leg and nervous system are all narrowed to one task, to which the whole attention is also constrained—the pursuit and pulling down of specific prey. But the embryonic wolf is not such a streamlined fang. Indeed here we see the ancestral type, an altogether rounder and more all-round creature, more rounded especially in skull and brain—in fact approximating to that all-round unspecialized type which once, before the canine stock became wolfish, still possessed generalized response and a wide, if vague, awareness. In spite of that the wolf stock made the fatal choice—specialized efficiency in preying on the weak, instead of interest, wonder and mutual aid. That step can only be described as a Fall—a fatal departure down to violence and to the fate of the violent, death.

It was a fatal failure—but not quite, not for all and every branch of the wolf family. For it is here precisely that we come upon this strange redemptive process of taming, redemptive taming, through being brought to share house and life, work and trust with one who did not fall (at least not yet) into the fatal parasitism of specialization. After some millions of years of wandering, literally, in the wilderness, the snarling wolf-dog crept nearer the two fearful mysteries—man and his hearth. The still-latent trust and wonder in the cur made it grateful for kindness. The child, whom it would have devoured, became a creature whom it guarded as it would guard its own young. So the domesticated wolf-dog has been led back again, and not merely to wild freedom which, we see, would only be a return to that mental prison in which the wolves and all the carnivores have landed themselves. The dog has been led back by what it is not sentiment but precision to call the miracle of creative love, courageous love, self-forgetful interest-affection. He has been brought back to that age-long-ago epoch of his real freedom, of which the foetal wolf shows us a sign and the fossils of a score million years ago tell us a little further. First his temper, his emotion, was changed to trust: from trust springs patience, the power of trustful attention and the desire to please. From these arises wonder. Next the intelligence takes fire from the emotions and understanding is awakened. Finally, most striking proof of re-creative power, physique itself responds to the new, re-created demands of the new psyche, the reborn soul. In the Pomeranian dog and other similar strains, we have a renewed animal, a creature with a rerounded skull and the fuller brain that goes with this: a beast no longer suited even by its frame to be a pursuing parasite, dominated by simple, destructive reflexes, a creature that could not survive if banished back to such a life but one who can "fit in with" the varied environment of a human home, share its interests and emotions, respond to and yield affection, in short, be a symbiotic member, a partner of a household. Such a creature is then doubly free. Collar and kennel are not for it. Its nature having become integrated with its master's, it is free of all he has. It goes as it will, for its will has found a fullness of life with him, beside which wildness was captivity. "His service is perfect freedom." Yet because of this re-creative affection, its vitality is not weakened; its courage is increased. Nearly all wild beasts are natural cowards. Fear is their lifelong master, and lust and greed and even maternal affection are only momentary usurpers. The dog guarding his master or his home is as self-forgetfully brave as any human hero. Bravery therefore has been gained and beside bravery a new wonder. The dog is always aware, in its master, of a being who understands it and whom it understands to the immense fulfillment of its life, because, however faintly, it realizes the tremendous difference always present in the intimate association.

This example of psychophysical foetalization of the dog, of how the animal too can enter a new kingdom if it can become like a child and indeed be reborn—this case gives us a new light on what taming is and why the tamed must inherit the earth, why they alone can inherit it. For the future is only to them and for them. All the others, violent, triumphant beasts of prey though they seem, have already dug their grave with their own fangs. They are already moving, doomed sleepwalkers, down the last steps to the brink of extinction. And what is this clear example from domestic biology but a rendering in miniature detail of a vast, universal process of restorative renewal, the redemptive process which is the heart of religion? We must be born again; be made again as a child. The child's innocency, openness, wonder are not its distinctive characteristics—rather these are symptoms of this deeper thing. Indeed that thing is not so much a characteristic as a certain quality of consciousness itself. It sees the world without that narrowed focus which perceives that here is something to be exploited. It gazes without realizing that it itself is different, defensively different, from that on which it is looking with intuitive interest.

The promise of this Beatitude is then this double one: Firstly, you can be trained and then you will go on and be tamed. First you will be a servant and then "by adoption" a close friend, a child. Then, in that second stage you will no longer simply take the divine commands; you will begin to partake of the divine nature. Yes, and that nature will not remain simply in the mind. The body itself will respond and resonate with the New Life. To give that new life adequate flow, and under the shaping of that inflowing current, the physical frame itself becomes the lit temple of the Light, of the Holy Ghost; the physique is sanctified and illuminated by the redeemed psyche.

This, however, is to glance on to the goal, to the final Beatitudes, when the Children of God see Him and are united with Him. Here we must pause a moment and, going back to training and then to the task of earth inheriting, we must inquire further how that higher training will give us the new apt force to inherit the earth. It has become evident that it adds just two things to the training of the gallant and skilled fanatic, the devoted man of intense but limited loyalty. He has the secondary virtues. There are only two primary virtues: indeed it is one, because we see its unity under two aspects. It is that staunchless, dauntless, unlimited sympathy which is the understanding of the heart and that undisturbed, unbaffled understanding which is the sympathy of the mind. Interest and affection are the outgoing and returning tides of its being: interest which finds itself "being in" that which has called it out, and, in turn, affection which finds itself "affected," moved, touched, altered by that to which it has responded. He who has let these tides of Being begin to cleanse the stagnant pool of his self, begins to realize that, with the completion of each of these cycles of these cleansing waters "at their priestlike task of pure ablution," the sand bar of restricted understanding and sympathy is being washed away and he himself is being carried every tide out onto further oceans of Life, until he understands there is no loss, no drowning of the self in a sea of utter otherness, but that out here is true Being, his true Being. He suddenly understands, as it were by remembering, that he is "that which drew from out the Boundless Deep" and that he now "turns again home." He is not the banking of silt and sand which made the trapped water into a pool, a puddled travesty of the "pomp of waters unwithstood," he is the water, only able to know its real nature when moving freely and one with the universal flood.

That is the goal, that is the final magnificent maneuver whereby all alienness is embraced, enveloped, and overcome. This tide and this alone can rise to such height that it can overbrim the highest walls of suspicion, and flood and fill, percolate, saturate and inundate the widest, bitterest desert of resentment and cynicism. Some two thousand five hundred years ago one of the wisest of men whom we call Lao-tzu, looking out over a civilization scorched, blasted and fissured by passionate resentments, intense fanatic devotions, saw the same single solution. So he takes and uses as the simile for this percolating, solving power, this idea of water. It is, he tells us, always lowly, always, and of its great nature, seeking the lowest place, always working silently, patiently. Yet in the end, hard and rigid things yield to it. It works its way past frontiers, under dividing walls. It melts rock and carries away the proud hills which we call eternal, in its gentle flow. Yes, it remains when they have vanished. Another later poet looking at the ruins of Rome, the city which its citizens had called eternal, cries with the pang of semi-understanding, as he saw the huge imperial monuments settling into dust and the tumbling swirling yellow Tiber still flowing as it flowed before Romulus gathered mud for his first village:

> See here how fortune reigns
> The unmoved wanes
> And that which is forever passing on
> Remains.

But how are our rigid, restricted, withered little natures, stiff in their limited convictions, desiccated in their brittle pride, to become so supple, lithe, fluid? How are we to learn, as Lao-tzu prophesied, as the Beatitudes promise, to become unself-conscious, unimpatient parts of that great principle of dynamic transforming Acceptance; which bears so profoundly with all, in all, under all, that to call it tolerant is quite inadequate; which is so patient that our word patience is impertinent to describe its inexhaustibility; which is so kind that our notions of friendliness, in comparison with it, are crude and almost aggressive? This Heaven, this Divine Eternal Fatherhood, this which Lao-tzu calls Tao, the Everlasting Principle, that Law of Love, the very nature of Reality, which Buddha called the Dharma, that Being who as Dante saw, turns the sun and the stars, simply because He is Love, inexhaustible, compassionate Power, how shall *we* find that Power, that one and only apt and adequate Force? How shall we be trained so as not to thwart that creative light but to let it pour through us? True, it is nigh us.

To repeat again that dawn scripture, that inspired wisdom which has been speaking since that first Bible, the Upanishads, "He who is the centre of the sun, know thou, he is that in the core of thy heart." True, but even as we recognize the truth of those inspired words our heart must cry with that honest striving saint Anselm: "How far am I from Thee, who art so nigh to me!" Yes, it is only a step but it is that immeasurable step from Time to Eternity. It needs only one word to say it and be free, but we stammer and stutter and cannot get it out. In short, though the charisma, the sudden descent of the Paraclete, the sudden falling of the veil, is in a moment, to win to that moment, we must train. It is a culmination of an entire process. Then, once the small self is possessed, once the separation is over, the bonds sundered, then the person has become the Being. Then he has, or rather is possessed of, that inexhaustible resource which never is outmatched and overcalled; then he is made of that impersonal suppleness and incompressible strength which is water's strange two-sided power; then he is that easy unhurried incessant percolating influence. "He works," says Lao-tzu, "without working"; he is prodigiously active without exertion, persuasive without argument, eloquent without phrases, forceful without violence, without coercion, without pressure. He is always unnoticed but influential, unurgent but decisive, unconsulted but ordering.

Are these words merely faint echoes of the quaint ancient paradoxes of Chinese detachment? Or, however stumblingly, do they refer to a fact, so vast, so universal and pervading, that we have overlooked it, and hence have come into our acute confusion? Words can never prove facts unknown to the reader. Is there a training? That word at least is definite—it does not refer to any fancy, any sudden whim but to hardly, persistently won accomplishment. Is there a training whereby we might be filled with this high radiation, which unnoticed penetrates all and transforms all? The next Beatitude, it seems, refers to that. If we will own that we have nothing in ourselves: if we will allow that we need filling with another kind of force more different from what we have called forcefulness, might, power, than is the cosmic radiation different from black powder, then we may get it. We shall have to be certain, however, that we do want it, to know we have lost our way. We shall have to be certain beyond any doubt that nothing else will do and that come what will—yes, whether we strike it or no—we are determined to give all we have to find if there may be a path. That is to hunger and to thirst after righteousness, to long with one exclusive desire to find the way. It is with that creative longing that the next stage is concerned.

# V.

## PROFICIENCY—iii

### *The Creative Desire*

+++++++++++++++++++++++++++++++++++++++++++++

*"Blessed are they that hunger and thirst after righteousness: For they shall be filled."*

This fourth Beatitude, do what we will, must seem something of a letdown, if not an anticlimax. We started with the poor in spirit (if we could find them) being possessors of the Kingdom of Heaven. You have only to find a type, which, at first glance at least, should be numerous enough. Find these, stay among them until your eyes clear and you will see they have it, the Kingdom is their climate. Of course closer inspection quickly showed that complete holy poverty of spirit is very rare, is a very high attainment. Indeed, though it is the first thing we must try, it is not fully achieved until nearly all the other rungs of the Ladder of Beatifying Perfection have been scaled. Being able to feel intensely for others, it then became clear, is a very necessary step for us, if we are ever to escape from ourselves. We learn not only to feel but how and what we ought to feel—the dauntless compassion which, daring to face all sorrow, past present and future, daring to accept the whole of

[78]

Life and its tragedy, is comforted, is given both strength and vision, seeing the end and knowing the way.

These instructions taken, it seemed we were about to be let get to work and begin to rise straight away in executive power, in making practical contribution to ordering the actual world. Yet here again it became apparent that a great deal of preparation was still required of us. The earth would be inherited by the tamed: as soon as they were ready it would be at their disposal. Training, however, is an immense task of reconditioning. All the obvious, quick-production trainings are already being used, are turning out scores of thousands of disciplined devotees—and the world is certainly not becoming better ordered, let alone a Kingdom of Heaven. It is clear that, though the rigid self-sacrifice, crusading zeal, fanatic devotion of the best Communist, Fascist and Nazi simply cancel out and make chaos, nevertheless the best of these zealots do live a life which in its austerity, contempt for physical comfort, bodily courage and single-mindedness looks unattractively advanced to the average self-centered man. It is going to be difficult to equal in a good cause the selfless energy which many of such types have shown in a sorry one. It is going to be very difficult to produce a devotion of a higher quality, to produce for the noblest aim those noblest means which can alone attain it.

But, it may be asked, granted all that, granted that the training will have to be both very exacting and very wonderful, how is this going to be helped

by the text of this fourth Beatitude, by just hungering and thirsting after Righteousness? In the concluding sentences of the last discussion on the third
Beatitude, it was suggested that hungering and
thirsting after Righteousness might be rendered as
longing with one exclusive desire to find the Way.
Can that really give us the equipment we require
to give order to the earth? True, to most of us, long
used to regarding the words of Christ as far too
sacred to have any precise sense, let alone order, we
have taken for granted that this Beatitude returns
to holy uplift. After the last had fluttered into
paradox, a flutter which years of familiarity had
damped, until (long ceased to be thought of as true)
we do not even question whether it is untrue, after
that sudden mention of the earth and public concern, we return again to private piety, those unreal
interests of the ineffective good. Righteousness we
are certain we know—the self-righteous are an unpleasant pretentious lot. They live a life which is
unreal and protected and from their coign of conscience look down to tell the men who do the world's
work, delving, ditching and draining, that their
hands should be cleaner, their working style less
violent, their language sweeter.

That word Righteousness is, however, an elderly
one. It has gotten that middle-age spread and
flabbiness that affects words as much as people. It
was once shapely and keen. Righteousness was quite
specific once. It had precise meaning. The original
bones of the word show that, under the superfluous
flesh centuries of gush have wished on it. It is Right-

wise-ness. It is not a word dealing with vague distant prospects, sunset sunbursts, delectable mountains which may turn out to be clouds. It is a sound, hard-working term—not padding for perorations. Right-wise-ness is simply the right way of doing a thing, the right path for leading to a desired goal. As "likewise" means "similarly" so Right-wise means rightly, going the right way, to get the desired result, instead of the wrong.

With that vital word in this Beatitude made definite, it looks as though this Beatitude's connection with the last becomes clear and effectual. We have not turned aside from the earth and the problem of possessing it and giving it order. Having viewed our objective, having seen that only one type, the highest type of trained person, is ever going to inherit it, strict, causally related argument compels us to this next step—the finding of the precise technique, the appropriate skill, the right way of becoming trained.

Yet, even then, with that key word cleared, the Beatitude remains difficult. We want, we must have a super-skill, a technique of genius. That surely, if it is to be won at all, will, first, be by careful research in all methods of psychophysical training. Discipline and drill have been developed along with organization and instruments. The man needs to be reconditioned every time the machine is improved. That is Taylor's famous industrial principle. It is the reason why in good workmen, skill is prized above everything, above energy and willingness and even interest. Skill is knowledge which has spread not merely into the hands—so that artisans are called hands—but into those extension hands, those extrapolated limbs which we call our instruments.

Soldiers, concerned with the utmost force, the most violent pressure, that of men flung at one another, have for millennia been concerned with the problem of the man and the machine, and the need that they be one, if an effective weapon is to be forged. Each change in armament has required as radical a change in discipline, in drill. That is why the rapid advances in weapons, which modern invention has allowed, have been anything but welcome to the pure soldier; as little as to a chess master would be sudden changes in the values and powers of his chessmen. The discoveries how to condition large masses of normal individual men to act under fire as one mass, and to obey one order, however repugnant it might seem to their individual bodies, minds and souls, those inventions were mainly made by the Swede ideological leader Gustavus Adolphus. Every advance in firearms ever since had presented a problem to those whose master recipe for conditioning men dated from times when death machines were in their infancy. The Duke of Wellington was not a blind old reactionary when he refused to have the British army supplied with rifled muskets. He declared that with his long knowledge of the subconscious habit factors on which an army's discipline depended, any radical change in armament, and so in the inured routine of drill, would be too dangerous to the men's morale even if balanced with greater accuracy of fire.

Now, granted that it is getting incomparably more difficult than in the Iron Duke's day to keep the drill, the discipline, abreast with the death machines; granted that, increasingly, the aim of modern drill is not to create a creature of conditioned reflexes incapable of thinking for itself, but on the contrary, the intensely difficult problem, of creating a man of two parts, one incapable of thinking *of* himself, but always capable in uncomparably strange, unforeseen circumstances, of thinking *for* himself, of being quite detached in mind and absolutely attached in emotions; granted that is the practical issue militarist and democrat have to face, what is the solution? More and more independence must be given the individual soldier. There is no way out of this surprising denouement. We have appealed to the Caesar of mechanism and we must go as it dictates, not as any human tyrant may wish. We face the paradox that it is the machine, blind and invariable, which has forced back on the mind of man the initiative which he thought he had lost for good. That line of future development is becoming clear to all men who have, as men in key positions must do today, to think straightaway and as far as they can see.

Hence the whole issue of training is rushing back into the focus of our thoughts, from which focus we thought, if we were to be realistic, the machine had banished it permanently to a secondary place. Hence the great and growing interest in all practical skills of the mind, in methods of making the body, the nervous system, the subconscious mind to obey the surface will. This is only a wave today: it will be a spring tide tomorrow. Hence when we find religion talking about mind-training, the physical disciplines necessary for it, the effects it produces, the technical knowledge you need to do it, the difficulties and dangers resulting, quite a new welcome awaits such remarks. We are suddenly willing to listen to discussion we should a few years ago have dismissed as dull nonsense. More than half the considerable interest now shown by respectably intelligent people in Mysticism today has its roots in this—the realization that here and here alone might lie the power to master the runaway machine.

Well, here is the point where the Beatitudes seem to be bearing upon what is already an anxious interest, and may soon be little short of an obsession. This clause, which we thought was vague and private, is of pressing and public concern. "What does it tell us," we ask with growing impatience, "about the training that will give us the proper mastery, apt force, real preservative power? Surely there is such technical knowledge to be found and to be acquired. We are ready. We own we must have it. Let us know and let us be taught to practice." That demand is swelling. It springs from a clear and arresting realization that we simply must have an apt force and not this grotesque hypertrophy of violence which now works less well than a dynamite cartridge would work to adjust a chronometer. It springs also from a realization which any initial study of Mysticism reveals, that such force is known and such training can be acquired. Then we turn to the Beatitude which speaks of the Right Way of being trained and of mastering the machine and all the earthly blind forces. What does it say? We are daunted. We are just to hunger and thirst after the way and we shall find ourselves full of it, we shall find the technique discharging, as it were, from our finger tips?

Surely such a conclusion shows that the whole of the deduction must have been wrong, that this Beatitude, whatever it means, has really nothing to do with the Beatitude which came before it, with being trained? Are we then to treat it and dismiss it as simply a piece of good advice, a verse that tells us no more than it is good to be good and if you want it enough you will get it? That choice, that interpretation is certainly debarred. But the alternative, which says this clause is dealing with and developing the issue brought out in the clause before, and is telling us how to be people adequate to be the inheritors of that immense mortgaged estate, the earth, how to be the competent receivers of the bankruptcy of mankind, that alternative reading is certainly not obvious.

We must then go more deeply into this problem or we must leave it as an irrelevant platitude. We have seen that large and increasing numbers are ready, and far more are being made ready, to accept the idea that psychological training, which fundamentally alters character, is both possible and now necessary. But these numbers who are ready to open or reopen the question of character changing, still carry over from the bankruptcy of mechanism certain of its assumptions. One of the most distinctive of these is the belief that the will has very little decisive power in any changes which really matter, in this case, such changes as could affect radically a man's psychophysical makeup. True, the will decides that such steps, if possible, shall be taken. After that, however, the process must be scientific, i.e., it must be a process which will work, like arsenic poisoning or a stiff dose of alcohol, whether you co-operate or not.

Now, it must be allowed and should be, that there appear to be some striking techniques and methods of mind-body training which, provided the intelligence carries out the instructions, the processes can take place, the results follow, regardless whether the individual in question feels strongly about it or no. If for example you can disturb any of the main ductless glands in your body, you will of course feel physical and emotional changes taking place in your mind-body whether you desire these states or not. This is an important distinction to make clear for, there can be no doubt, we shall soon see certain psychophysical methods in ever more general use and producing ever more striking results. Striking, yes, but whether desirable is another question. The point which we can make clear, and must, is this: such methods have nothing to do with spirituality or perhaps one should say, no more than high explosives. They may add to efficiency, they will not and cannot add to real understanding. They can aid our present enthusiasms, they cannot enlarge us into that dynamic love which must embrace mankind. They are, then, incapable of giving us what we are peremptorily demanding—mastery of the runaway machine and power which will yield us so apt a force and influence, that we may overcome the chaotic forces at present wrecking the world. In short, every change made without a new devotion and dedication of the will, is made not in the ends but only in the means. Even if we make it in our bodies and brains it is still external to ourselves, still material, still only adding to that already capsizing side of the balance, to our powers and not to our understanding, to our old fatal passions instead of to a real change in character.

That then would seem the reason for this sudden concentration in this Beatitude on desire, on an overmastering exclusive will. At a stroke, we are swept back from the wide vision of the world inherited by the trained, back to the question of ourselves, our will. Do we really want the world saved? If so, how much do we want it? It can be done, but the price is definite. Any other sum will not be accepted. We see the world has been refused to men who did give much of themselves, men who often said they would stick at nothing. They did of course stick at one thing—giving themselves. They gave their time, their energy, their comfort, their blood, their friendships, their principles, but, like Ananias, they held back part of the price, their wills. So, soon they killed each other. Now we are on the threshold of being able to release more power, liquidate ever more of ourselves to yield higher efficiency, apt force. But for what? True, mechanized militarism is a clumsy instrument, so clumsy that all who want to produce any intended result, to attain any rational definite objective, will soon be abandoning this monstrous imprecision. And then, with official war officially dead we shall "live happily ever after!"? Alas, it is not as simple as that. For, observe, it is not the idealists and pacifists who are, by their actual behavior, pressing forward the elimination of war. Paradoxical as it seems, it is the dictatorships not the democracies which have taken the initiative here. Mechanization, compelling the militarist to develop any weapon regardless of consequences, has had the most unsuspected consequences. At the two ends of the militaristic front the development of two forces have combined to destroy frontiers and liquidate nationalism. The bombing plane and radio propaganda dissolve all fronts and aim indiscriminately at everyone. The higher the explosive and the wider the broadcast the less is there any respecting of persons or estimate of results.

The Dictators already sense this and so have already prepared to shift from the self-stultifying hypertrophy of violence—to more apt, more precise methods. But not to better. What are the new instruments of forceful precision, of exact pressure, of real direct action? They are those which bear straight upon the will. We have been so obsessed with violence on the grand (but ineffective) scale, so shocked by large-scale mechanized slaughter, that we have failed to see that this is now a bypath leading to a blind alley. Indeed the main arterial track diverged some time ago. It was Clausewitz, one of the patron saints and doctors of militarism, who taught that the soldier must never be distracted from his one central objective—the will of the opposing commander. All present mechanized militaristic methods, such as great guns so big that they fire blindly into the stratosphere and planes bombing from 30,000 feet and more, try to justify their lack of aim by saying that whomsoever and whatever they may accidentally damage, contribute to "lowering the enemy's morale."

Such an argument is a clumsy defense of clumsiness. The dictatorships, hard and radically as they worked at war, worked far more radically at official war's superseder. That is a new flexible front composed of the secret police, propaganda, "conditioning" education and scientific torture. Ever since the G.P.U., in the service of a new persecution, took up the research and experiment which ceased with the Inquisition, there has been rapid unadvertised progress in learning how to break the will without the indirect method of breaking the body. Each year are made new discoveries in technique and precision of application. We now know the exact damp heat which makes the will flaccid; how repeated electric shocks of a certain voltage shake resolution far quicker and more profoundly than any scourging; how certain hours of sleeplessness leave the door of the mind swinging open helplessly, its careful secrets exposed. A stubborn man can be changed in a week or less into one so pliable

[89]

that he will own to faults he never committed, ask for his own punishment and denounce his friends. He will even remain so conditioned for longer and longer periods. Final triumph of apt force, precise violence, no mark can be found on the body, no trace of physical damage.

Does it seem out of place to discuss modern secret police methods in an essay on Christ's teaching? It is not. He who was concerned above all else with the human will, to him such discoveries are surely of interest. "He that planted the ear shall He not hear?" He that drew out the nerve fibers shall He not understand human suffering? It is vitally necessary to draw attention to this development, for we are in great danger of taking to these methods. So pleased shall we be that open war has gone, so ignorant of real spiritual force, so anxious to applaud any force which is not hopelessly inaccurate and inept, that we shall overlook the fact that evil remains evil, indeed becomes if anything more evil, the more it is efficient. Efficiency is not virtue: it is simply a neutral magnification of evil or of good. As Christ always taught, all evil is in the will, the act is merely an echo. To break a man's will quietly behind walls, in a place which can, if you like, be called a hospital and not a prison; without losing your temper to make a man lose his conscience, his sense of right, his God-given reason; to watch him quietly with dispassion; to treat him daily till you know his every refuge and hold; to continue until he collapses; that is surely in God's eyes a more evil thing than to rush blindly at

another you have never seen and in animal excite.
ment try to kill him.

That issue put plainly, we can go back to our
text with a new if terrible light upon it. Today's
contemporary progress in apt force, precise violence,
makes it painfully clear why any advance in training, any switch over from physical force to psychological force, will only leave us nearer hell. The
evil spirit of physical violence may be driven out
but unless the empty, ordered house is to be possessed by God Himself then the evil spirit will return with these other horrors seven times worse
than itself. For they are able to pollute the wells
and sanctuaries of man's soul, to which clumsy
physical violence could seldom penetrate.

So if we would avoid tumbling into this trap we
must know clearly why we want a new technique
of training and a new world. For what, for whom?
The only safe answer, though it sounds extreme,
is for God. That precisely is why this Beatitude
follows the one before. First and foremost we must
fix and focus the will. We must want, until we want
nothing else, the right way—to be filled completely
with the one wish, this one yearning, as the migrat-
ing bird has only one desire in all its being. We
must want the way, the whole way, not a smart
step to give us "the start of the majestic world."
Everything, we now realize, turns upon the will—
not merely what we do and what we think—but
even how much of the world we see. Knowledge
depends on will. It is the striving wish to apprehend
more than we can see, that permits us to see more.

All our senses develop if they are used and atrophy if unused. It seems that they all started from a deep striving and craving to grasp the outer world.

We must desire passionately, wholly, only, to find the way out. We must understand what Christ meant in saying that the Kingdom is a pearl of great price, to purchase which every other asset and security is liquidated. We must attend to what Buddha meant when he vowed that he would die in his tracks unless he could find the path of Deliverance, the way of Life. We must recall the story sometimes told of him that when he had found the way and thousands were flocking to him, one man coming into his presence was told to follow him— for it was bathing time—to the river. Thinking this meant a ritual purification, the seeker gladly followed. As soon, however, as they were at some depth in the stream, he found himself pushed under and held, until at his last gasp, with a desperate wrench, he forced his head above water. To the quiet question, "When you thought you were going to be drowned, what did you desire most?" he gasped with some exasperation, "Air!" "When you want salvation as much as you wanted air," came the reply, "then you will get it."

The newborn child has often to be shocked and shaken into using its new and painful lungs. It has long depended for its life on another's breathing. Now the cord is cut, breathe or suffocate it must. So must we gasp for the Breath of Life. If we are to live, and our human society to live, we must start this new circulation; break through the suffocating membrane of the self. That is the way. The first step is, then, not a great knowledge of techniques. Effective and powerful though they may be, they are neutral, serving death or life as we direct our way either to death or to life, either to the devil or to God. They can only take us to the devil if our nature, because of its uneradicated egotism, still refuses to point to God. Direction is primary—it is the will to find God; to be on the way to God that is fundamental. Then, seeking the Kingdom of God, all other things, all the equipment—and it is much—for reaching that Kingdom, for putting it within the reach of others—are added. Then we can learn safely about apt force, psychological training, spiritual power. The tremendous exclusive desire has broken us out of the shell of the self; we are wrenched out of that vicious circle which eddies round—from bad means (employed because by our former using of them we have blinded ourselves to any other) leading to bad ends calling for further evil methods. In short we have decided first and foremost, to find God, to find whether He really demands that we do evil that good may come, to seek for Him if necessary till we die, to refuse the lure of any pursuit or goal, (however good it may sound so long as it demands a doubtful means) until we have found Him and found the answer to that question.

It is that tremendous suction caused by the vacuum of the self, it is that total desire, which draws in the answer of the positive power. For with that "last gasp" we really at last begin to live. With that birth pang we are delivered into the real and eternal life. We find ourselves linked up in a vast circulatory system whereby, through us and our fellows, flows out the love of God, passes, in reciprocating processes from man to man and so brings them back again to God. How those live, function and create, when, by such desire, they have become part of the Eternal Life, the next Beatitude discovers.

# VI.

## PERFECTION—i

### *The Recreative Mercy*

✛✛✛✛✛✛✛✛✛✛✛✛✛✛✛✛✛✛✛✛✛✛✛✛✛✛✛✛✛✛✛✛✛✛✛✛✛✛✛✛✛✛

*"Blessed are the merciful: for they shall obtain mercy."*

Those words at least confirm the last deduction from the former Beatitude. A cycle, a reciproca-tory process is being described. A process of results, of getting what you give, reaping what you sow, a rhythm, which began with the craving for the right way, is now well started. Indeed, that beat began—like the heartbeat of the chick when still in the egg—even when we were at the second Beatitude, when the mourners find they are com-forted, when sorrow has led to vision and the strength to pursue the vision.

But the cycle is not a closed circle. These Beati-tudes have been likened to rungs on a ladder. It would be an exacter simile to say that they resemble more closely that curious escalator, the Archimedes screw pump. In that device, water is drawn up by revolving a slanted spiral tube, the water flowing without break—always falling but always also ris-ing—from one coil to another, until, what was scooped up from the river, is emptied out high up on the bank above. So, in the ascent of the Beatitudes we both rise by a continual process of dynamic humbling, what has been called by some moralists "falling up stairs," and also, each stage is not sharply divided from the next—we pass into one as we proceed out of the other.

Here, we must take note of the particular stage that we are now entering, the upper half of the entire evolution. We have completed our self-training. We have become proficients. We have acquired the three essential proficiencies: (1) that of diagnostic insight, of seeing sorrow and the ending of sorrow; (2) that of being trained, tamed, re-natured, made companions of the household of God; (3) and finally—more essential than the acquiring of a new true insight or even new right habits—new desire, new appetites. We are trained, we are proficient and adept right down to our basic cravings and reflexes. We are a new creature. That new creature, being wrought in ourselves, God can at length work through us to cause the whole creation to be redeemed. Now, having prepared a pure strain of leaven, of yeast, this strain may be worked in with the mass of dough and the whole lump be leavened.

Therefore at this fifth Beatitude we enter, of necessity, on the work of perfection, on the creative task of the Perfect. We have only two more levels and they, as we saw at the beginning, are so high and comprehensive that we may almost say that they are interchangeable, or two aspects of the same complete final state. But at this present level of the fifth Beatitude we have already reached the point where the creative communion of God and man has begun to come into manifest play. It is as though, through those first four stages, a storage process had been going on. Man has been first emptied and then, with the battery cell cleaned and ready, it has been linked up with the dynamo to be recharged. Now something like an adequate charge has been accumulated. Now a current begins to flow back again to the source which replenished it.

As when a thunder storm is high, besides the lightnings stabbing down from the clouds, answering flashes leap up to the clouds from the earth, so man, when he is filled with God, may reply to God. That is the doctrine of Immanence, of God being authentically within us. It is an essential side of the supreme truth and mystery, the Nature of God as far as we may apprehend it. If we let go of this idea and truth of Immanence, then God is lost to us. We say it saves His majesty not to pollute His Light with our dust. Quite apart from the abstract question whether God can be "polluted" whatever we do, the vital practical matter is that, though by making God utterly transcendent we believe we are honoring Him, making Him the Object of supreme adoration, we are actually shelving Him. There can be no doubt that that is what happens whenever God's Transcendence is stressed so as to deny His constant, most intimate Immanence. But equally if we hold to Immanence and lose Transcendence we find ourselves left with no God, only a constantly diminishing good will, a constantly shrinking inspiration.

Man can reply to God but it is a reply, an answer

to a call, an increment or interest earned from a given fund, from a bestowed capital. Man must reply to God, must, when stirred within, seek ever further out; or the inner voice will be silenced. That inner voice, at first man can only know as a strange silent friend, patient to the degree that, beyond a hint, the voice scarcely ever is heard unless it is asked to speak, its opinion waited for. Overspeak it, disregard it and soon we become unaware that we have any companion; we laugh off the notion; for, after all, it is not reassuring to feel you are incessantly watched by an observer you choose not to consult and you suspect you do not please. We say conscience is all nurse's nonsense or superstitious people's substitute for secret police. If, however, we do not overrule what seemed at first no more than a whisper of restraint, a suggestion toward generosity, this voice grows in clarity, constancy and strength. For again we find that "as we open"—the inner ear—"it enters," until we hear, no longer a voice which we may mistake for self-suggestion and which could spring from self-will, but the Creative Word itself. We realize at last the completing Truth, the Truth which makes us free, that the voice speaking within the finally purified conscience is the Voice which called all creation out of the void; that the Spirit who created the Universe is the Spirit speaking in the heart emptied of self to be filled by Him.

This fifth Beatitude is dealing with the divine activity which takes place when the Immanence and Transcendence of God are realized as a reciprocal process, as indeed two dynamic aspects of the one and only Being. This is a profound mystery, as long as we try to comprehend it with an intellectual detachment and critical analysis. For we are dealing with the problem of Time and Eternity, how He that is Eternal and above all change can manifest Himself in the incessant flux of Time. Confronted with that riddle it is natural to take refuge in one solution or the other: either to let God's essential Being, that he is the Eternal, be lost, in order to hold on to the faith in His concern with us, His Presence in Time and in us, creatures of Time; or to let the fact of His omnipresence (which assures us of His Life in us) be sacrificed, in order to have the faith in His Eternity, in order to know, that, whether we fail, He can never pass.

But even as an intellectual proposition, even with our present reasoning powers, it is clear that if the word Transcendence means anything then it over-rules any, even the loftiest exclusiveness. God, because He is Transcendent, cannot be shut out of Time, "cannot be imprisoned in His Transcendence." Because of His Transcendence, He is eminently Immanent. We shall, however, never make any practical meaning and value of these polar words unless, instead of debating with them, we put them into action; making with them nodes, between which the current of life may flow. They cannot be for us definable concrete entities: they can be functions. In living spiritual issues—it must be repeated—we avoid much blind disputing and achieve new insight if we understand that we are using rather an algebra than an arithmetic.

This Beatitude mentions neither of those abstract words Transcendence or Immanence. But it is dealing with them, by telling us how to live so as to become those to whom such words have a real content. Mercy is the most practical path whereby anyone may learn about God for "like may only know like." The Godhead, who is so much beyond our minds as long as we are shut in them and ourselves, approaches our comprehension when we, by mercy, make contact with that aspect which of its Nature (because It is merciful) bends down to our inadequacy. "But," we stop and ask, "is not mercy too anthropomorphic? Is it not all too likely that as forgiving people is both socially necessary and individually most difficult, we have had to invent a divine sanction? Surely God, if there is a God, is above mercy far more than he is above justice. Justice is impersonal, inflexible, eternal law; but mercy is man's weakness, his sentiment, his failure to realize consequences and his wish to avoid the inevitable."

That argument carried more weight with our parents. We have discovered that so many of the laws they thought they had found were only associations they chose to make. We have seen that strict causality may be a rule of our minds: it cannot be established in outer nature, in phenomena. With every fresh scientific discovery we thought we were going to arrive at it, but always the clinching proof eluded us. And now what we were finding (and what it seems, we shall have to rest content in finding) is no more and no less than probabilities, the law of averages, the principle of chance.

So law and justice can claim no higher station in the categories of Truth than mercy and redemption. Nor in these Beatitudes is mercy introduced here at the fifth step with any randomness. This is not sentiment or casual uplift looking for a nice warm-feeling word, a word to encourage us to be nice to one another because it will pay us privately. Right-wise-ness, the way to the Kingdom, the path to Happiness, is through mercy. The only way the earth will be inherited and not devastated and depopulated is by mercy. For mercy is not, as in our hopeless moods we have imagined, something which we have to yield; which others, for social peace and pity's sake, implore us to yield; a foregoing of our right against someone who is wrong, incompetent, a drag, a waster, an unrelieved liability. Mercy is of the nature of things. The merciful of this fifth Beatitude are being educated, equipped, adapted and adopted to become the "Children" of the sixth. As we have seen, the great premise of the Beatitudes, their foundation in fact, their culmination in creative faith, is precisely that kindness is the core of creation. The Father of all, the Creator and Sustainer of everyone, is merciful to all. Without exception they are His Children whether they know it or not. And so those who recognize His nature and recognize their nature as His, do so by showing the same kindness, and by that kindness men know that such men are the Father's children—children who are growing in their godlike kindness until, transcending the limits of any self-regard, they become perfect, unlimited, as He is perfect, unlimited.

This clause of the Beatitudes seems central. If we look upon the seven sayings as a bridge rather than a ladder, a bridge spanning the gulf between man and God, Time and Eternity, then we may take this as the keystone of the arch. The abutment of this mighty span is that base and assembly line where the emptied-of-self are defined as those required. Here the raw material, the ore is stacked: the raw recruits mustered. Then we have two great preliminary sectors: the power of truth to face sorrow, the power of love to feel compassion. And, on the further side of the span we have the two great conclusive sectors: the service to man and recognition by man and the worship of God and transformation in God. Hence on this fifth Beatitude the whole structure pivots. The same thing has been noticed in that other quintessence of instruction and training, the Lord's Prayer. There, at its center, are the two clauses, the first on the reconditioning of the soul by the new diet, the Bread of the Coming Day and the second, that reciprocation of re-creation through forgiving and being forgiven.

Forgiveness and being forgiven, being merciful and being shown mercy—they are the two sides of the great wheel or spiral of spiritual ascent. The merciful acknowledge their union with those whom they could, by earthly standards, safely disown. Justice would permit the division, but mercy, seeing deeper, will not. Justice divides justly but mercy reunites creatively. The one fault of justice is that it is mechanic. It can cut asunder exactly: it cannot bind up, heal and make grow. It shows people how best they may cut loose of each other's grapple, go off apart, cease girding and grasping at one another.

But mercy says there is no solution in sundering, because all our pain and striving arises from our failure to realize that we are one. And because the merciful acknowledge their kinship with those who have let them down, God acknowledges, by this their act, His kinship with them, and they, and those they have drawn to them, are drawn up.

The process, it is clear, is not done in a moment, for this is a vast redemptive cycle. As we show mercy we are granted more mercy. This is not merely a restorative act: it is much more. It is not simply putting things back into place, a reordering of a disarranged tidiness, putting neatly right a pattern which has been overset. Justice is always attempting to do that, to treat each case, each subject, each person on his own, as a separate wholly responsible individual. Justice can never deal adequately with Life because it is always thinking in dead terms, is always trying to arrange everyone in a mechanic orderliness and to get them so to stay. They cannot, because they are all parts of Life. Their legal frontiers, the demarcations which justice draws between man and man, between your responsibility and your irresponsibility are unreal, untrue. The invisible fibers of influence, affection, social pressure, conflicting loyalty, weave and warp our single strands; and all the threats and appeals of justice to our self-concern through reward and punishment cannot make us keep in place.

Are we then to relapse into anarchy and let all the strands fall in tangle, all the tendrils of Life's Tree writhe upon and strangle one another? There is a third way: not to try to arrest life, nor to try to let it go back, but to draw it on and out. That is the way of creative mercy. Mercy, we must repeat, is much more than sparing an enemy, relinquishing a stranglehold on a debtor. As forgiveness is a great upward moving spiral, forgiveness of wrongs done to the self, of wrongs done to others, of the wrong woven into the web of Life itself, so too is Mercy. But while forgiveness only begins its action when wrong has been done, is the repairing reaction to injury, the "governor" on the engine of Life, restraining after the engine has begun to race and strain, Mercy is more vigilant, more initiative, more original. The Lord's Prayer which is training us, naturally begins where we are, at the problem that confronts us, the problem that we have wronged, run up debts and trespassed and also we have been wronged, hold bad debts and have been trespassed against. But the Beatitudes, as they are the next, more advanced stage, in them the preservative virtue of forgiveness is raised to the creative inspiration of mercy.

Here we see the creative power of God shown through His instrument or lens, dedicated man. God made a perfect creation; his primal creative act established a universe which was very good. The supreme achievement of that universe was to make possible a creature who should have creative power. That involved giving the creature the divine power of freedom, for free will and creativeness are two words for one thing, for an act whereby the creature produces a radically new thing in the creation. He no longer simply rearranges what falls to him; he adds something that has never been present before. That gift must entail the possibility of failure, of power being used wrongfully, of the creative freedom being used by the separate spark of the individual, not to create more and grander and more perfectly integrating order, more unity, but a little system of its own and for its own. This is cosmic cancer.

The Supreme Creative Power, faced with this development can do three things. The obvious paths are either to quash the whole procedure, liquidate that which has failed to understand and to co-operate; or, by the superiority of overwhelming power, to coerce the subordinate creative individual, compelling him to come into line. These are obvious courses because they are the kinds of conduct which occur to our minds. Such policy is natural to us because it is anthropomorphic—the reaction of a magnified man. But God is not a magnified man and, further, were He so to act, all his design would have been a failure. The "Eternal" of His nature cannot fail. His creative power allows for all contingencies. Granted we act as He intends and we could and should, then we come to Him. Granted we act as we think serves our end, we can suffer and so learn. We cannot destroy His plan but only draw out, as it were, more creative power. We failing to go to Him, He comes to us.

So we must always remind ourselves that redemption is creation. Creation which began and set going the phenomenal universe, once again, when that universe is becoming evil, enters this time as Redemption. In consequence, because Redemption is creation, is God coming to man's help when man has proved inadequate as a creator, redemption is far more than restoration. A new richness is added to Life. Discords into which man had bungled and which were certainly beyond man's power to resolve, are taken up into a higher harmony. We come back again to the cry of Augustine and many other even loftier saints; the cry, "O Felix Culpa," "O happy fault," for it was through my failure that the supreme inexhaustible creative love found opportunity to achieve a redemptive creation, even more wonderful than that which was first and flawless. The deeper I fell, the more hideous the discord I created, the more astounding is the resolution of that discord into harmony, the more marvelous is the restorative recovery. It is not merely that I who seemed utterly lost am saved. Through the creative power which saves me, the whole universe is made the richer by this redemptive-creative act. So we may hope to understand why "there is more joy in Heaven over one Sinner who repents than over ninety-nine just men who have no need of repentance."

This is perhaps the deepest of mysteries and certainly one would guard against giving any impression that in these rudimentary words may have been given even a suggestion of evil's true nature. Yet such lines of thought, though explaining not at all the fundamental problem, may perhaps help toward our so living so that we may come where the issue is understood. So the saints encouraged themselves until they won to the answer, that answer which inspires life but adds not a word to argument. We may then complete the hypothesis of Redemption by pointing to its conclusion, a conclusion a number of mystic saints indicated. Evil, we must own, goes deep into Life. It is present not only in us but in our stock. I act ill not merely by my clear narrowed selfish choice for my personal advantage. I act ill by a deep drive which may have a terrible selflessness, an unself-seeking destructiveness—yes, self-destructiveness—inspiring it. That is original sin. But, further, evil is present in other stocks, breaking out, a common latent infection in all Life.

As has been suggested earlier in Chapter 3 on the second Beatitude, sin in its root nature would seem to be a shrinking back into a defiant pleasure, a defiant pleasure in the separateness of the self, a shrinking back which can take place (but can only take place) the moment that there is a consciousness of having attained a separate experience. That self, however dimly, does deliberately choose and decide to stay where it is; to resist all further growth; to regard all other contacts as intrusions, trespassers; to hug itself and to attack all else as alien. This is failure of vitality. Whether it shrink into a shell

[107]

and respond as little as a stone or whether it rush out with fangs and claws to devour and destroy, at root it is the same thing—a resolve not to co-operate, a determination to cling to oneself alone, a refusal to recognize the common life in itself and in all, a resolution to be in Life but not of it, to be an active or passive parasite.

Certainly this double process of degeneracy has appeared throughout Life's history from the earliest fossil records that we can trace. Indeed we may say that the Tree of Life as it rises is always shedding its leaves on one side or the other. Save for the one stock which gave rise to the mammals, all the vast processions and proliferations of Life up to that point seem to have made one or other of the two fatal choices—passive or active parasitism—timid or violent withdrawal. One strain and one strain only was able to avoid being overwhelmed either by greed or by fear, to choose, in however rudimentary a form, understanding and Love, so to pass the otherwise fatal threshold of the self and to emerge into a higher consciousness.

And once again, as the vast Phylum or Tree of Life reaches that station to which we belong—the third great level, that of warm-blooded life, we see at every one of these last stages the same drastic weeding out as, at level after level, type after type fails to sustain the constant effort of still fur-ther acceptance, still more awareness, still wider consciousness.

So as we have seen there first fell out those mam-mals who went so far back as to retreat again into the sea. They abandoned hand and land to become monster mouths, simple food scoops. That has been the fate of the entire whale family. Then the next level of animals to yield to the temptation to become nothing but browsers, the cattle, paid a price: their hands became hoofed. In turn the helplessness they had chosen turned them into a tempting prey for another stock. The carnivores appear: a degenerate reply to the temptations offered by another sort of degeneracy. Passive degeneracy provokes active degeneracy—the browsing parasite incites the devouring parasite. At this stage (geologically, the middle stage of the great Tertiary Epoch) the fate of all save one of the mammal stock is settled. All starting, as we too started, as a small handy creature, they have all chosen specialization and retreat. The one stock still left widely aware is the ape stock. But the apes, in turn, have through the last few million years been unable to resist this inner shrinking, this refusal to continue to accept. They are all now living fossils. The foetal ape is a more unspecialized creature than the newborn animal. Already in the womb, the ape of today has begun to degenerate. He is born doomed.

When therefore we would try to think upon evil and grasp its true, comprehensive nature, we must understand how long it has dogged life. Indeed we are driven to the conclusion, reached in an earlier chapter, when considering the sources of evil's cure, the origin of redemption, that as long as there has been life and as long as there will be life there must be present the temptation to treat the temporal as though it were the Eternal, to settle down, to shut off, to assert "As I am, I am sufficient in myself: I refuse to evolve further; I refuse to be included with the rest."

No, evil did not start with man. No, not with warm blood. The giant reptiles' bones are scored, pierced and rotted by disease. The giant reptiles evolved into types which tore and battened on each other. Here then our modern vision ranging back hundreds of million years has enlarged the tragedy and mystery. But here, too, if, as the mystics point out, redemption is creativeness, we may wonder with hope as to whether man's redemption, as it does so much more than restore him, does not also secure the release, the re-creation of all that baffled striving of which all life's history bears witness. We have seen that even the very moderate kindness of a human home has actually salvaged some of the wolves—the dogs are creatures which have been "foetalized," redeemed. The best animal tamers have said that there are no "dangerous animals." If only you know how to hold your initiative of self-forgetful interest and so to contact them, your complete lack of fear and greed, your complete possession by interest-affection allays their suspicion and awakes their response. The most dynamic saints, the men who both understood as well as felt the Eternal Life in themselves, they demonstrated the same thing even more strikingly—wild beasts sensing in them the creative, reassuring power, the irresistible kindness. The process of redemption by mercy does not stop with man but can extend to beast and indeed, the more we reflect upon it, we must ask, shall it stop there? Is not this kindness, the nature of the Father of all, is not this the secret of the redemption of all, of everything, through all being delivered from that illusion of the self?

Eckhart shows clearly that there are three great levels of sin and failure; states which separate us from God: first, our personal sins; then our inherited nature—"Is not He all save that which has power to say 'I am I'?"; and lastly, Time itself. If redemption is then creation, it re-creates us, first, in deed, individually, then in being, as a race, and finally the whole creation is released. It is separation that is the base of sin, as the essence of redemption is at-one-ment. Time is the great and fundamental sunderer. That is why Eckhart cries, "O Lord God we beseech Thee, deliver us from the life that is divided into the life which is united." That surely is the clear vision of the great mystic Paul when he cries, "The *whole* creation travails and groans— labours in birth pangs—waiting the emergence of the children of God."

We may hope then that we are not saved for ourselves. We have not been shown mercy just to be thankful, but to re-radiate the re-creative gift. So, too, in the Comprehensive Way—the larger vision of Mahayana Buddhism—the same thought is present; the same promise, a promise so splendid that the heart with its profound reason cries: "Here in some form, must lie the Truth." There it is taught that every perfected soul as it attains to the Light of all understanding, as it becomes through the

Divine Mercy completely released, turns back and stands incandescent with compassion, to light others on their way home. The freed soul acknowledges in the very discovery of its union with the Highest, its community with the lowest.

Mercy has of its very nature a great purity. For, as the Beatitude shows, it is not anything which starts up in the soul in order that the soul may save itself. We are shown by the structure of the fifth clause that it is speaking of those spirits who find themselves moved with compassion; we discover them moving toward man. The motion toward God has been traced in the four earlier Beatitudes. Now the return movement has begun the life of Union. But it is not a single self-completed cycle: it is a vast evolution. By being merciful the merciful obtain more mercy and as this mercy *is* deliverance from themselves they become able to show an ever more creative forgiveness, an ever wider, more dynamic compassion. They do not require the mercy for themselves: they would gladly be radiated away so that the light which streams on to them, the creative power, may pass through them intact, they themselves absorbing not a single photon. This is the great rhythm of mercy. We are rising to that scale whereon we may begin to sense the divine circulation of creative restoration, that vast tide which is always flowing. But by its very size and comprehensiveness it escapes us, as the incessant molecular activity in all liquids, even the stillest (shown by the "Brownian" movement) escapes our attention because it is too small.

On this Beatific Ladder of Perfection we have already attained a height when we can see those tides spreading to the confines of Life and the limits of Time. When from this lofty station we can see so far, we see that Time itself becomes not a misery but a mercy. It is no longer the denial of Eternity but an aspect of the Eternal. That is what Buddhism means when it says that to the completely liberated and enlightened soul, the soul which has become nothing but the Divine Compassion, this phenomenal world, this world which is appearance and illusion to the still struggling soul, becomes also Reality, "the Sangsara becomes Nirvana," the Kingdom of Heaven is come upon earth.

Such is the tremendous nature of mercy, for mercy—which perhaps we have dismissed as something amiable but weak—is revealed as nothing less than God the Creator seen actually working upon Time and in Time.

"In Time." The words echo with an overtone of stress and call us back like a warning bell from our high outlook to the actual moment. Is there time? Is it not very late still to be hoping? Will God, before it is too late, save his creature man from himself? It is the next Beatitude that describes specifically how that salvation is worked and the instruments which the Divine Mercy employs.

# VII.

## PERFECTION—ii

### *The New Creature*

✛✛✛✛✛✛✛✛✛✛✛✛✛✛✛✛✛✛✛✛✛✛✛✛✛✛✛✛✛✛✛✛✛✛✛✛✛✛✛✛✛

*"Blessed are the peace makers: for they shall be called the children of God."*

Last but one of the seven great Blessings this is the richest. All the others have been leading up to it, making it possible. Here is unfolded the Great Design, the culminating Purpose. But is not the seventh even greater? It has already been suggested that these two last Blessings are, as it were, one—two aspects of a single supreme state, a final condition of Pure Being. Certainly that which we have put last is the hardest to speak about. This sixth stage is surely lit with the Light of Heaven, but the Light is here being poured into Time, on to man. Hence, there results a rainbow of virtues, gifts, activities, the glowing spectrum of all the goodness, truth and beauty which can be expressed in the Manifold. The seventh looks straight into the Sun of Being itself—the prismatic belt passes back into that Clear Light of the Void which is Deity in that completeness of excellence that is "The One without a second," "He Who has no comparison." We must then, before we attempt to look at the culmination, see the splendor yielded even by its reflection. That at least gives us some conception of what its own inexpressible intensity must be.

In this sixth clause we are come to the point where the training is completed, the trained are manifested. They began by being Poor, Sorrowful, Meek, Hungry. What a college of cardinal virtues! The four abject states have been selected. The ground has been cleared, devastated, by failure of resources, failure of affections, failure of spirit, failure of stamina. What is left? We have seen; not simply an emptiness—quite the reverse—Proficiency. Everything that could be liquidated has been scoured off, eroded away, that there might remain in its nakedness that "ground of the soul" which, as Eckhart and all the great mystics say, ever remains one and indissolubly with and of God. That is the meaning behind the saying we so often misunderstand and misinterpret as just slackness, ceasing to trouble, letting go, the saying often used by the advanced mystics and the great artists. "All you have to do is to yield, to stop preventing creation coming through you." We can see now both how true that is and how completely different from any idle vacancy; what intensity of skilled strength is required to stay still and let God work on us. Then, with that living rock laid bare, on it there began to be raised the tower which, with no confusion or conflict of tongues, with no shift or give in its courses, can rise to Heaven. Here, in this stripped base of the soul, is that changeless elemental adamant which alone can be "that fulcrum which can move the world." Hereupon stand the merciful, receiving mercy and yielding mercy, until, with them as pivot, the love of God raises the most fallen of men, raises indeed the whole creation.

Now we are to see that work in its actual progress. The merciful we are told about in their relationship to God, we are told of that constant backing on which they rest—that, as they give, He keeps them perfectly reinforced. With this sixth Beatitude the viewpoint is reversed. Indeed up till now all the four foregoing promises have been something guaranteed by God as a gift from Him to those who have emptied themselves to receive. Suffering the loss of love they are given the Divine Comfort; suffering being tamed, God promises them the earth; hungry and thirsty with bafflement and frustration, longing to find the way, He promises that He will put them on it, will "guide their footsteps into the way of Peace." With this sixth, however, we hear another voice, we are told of another judgment. Even in the third blessing, when the earth was mentioned as reward of those meeked, trained, tamed; true the earth is to be given to them, but we are not told about what reception they will meet with from its inhabitants; how they are to get on; or even whether any of other mankind are to be left to share or serve in the new world. For all the text says the rest of the human race may have extinguished itself—a not impossible consequence of its present way of association—and the trained, the divinely domesticated species, alone survive. But now for the first time we hear a voiced opinion which shows that some others are on the scene, beside the trained and their Trainer, the disciplined disciples and their Master. The two sides of the clause, the statement and its explanatory reason, both point to the third party. The trained we see at their specific work; the merciful show particular activity and technique. They are Peacemakers.

Let us look at the first part of the clause first. We have seen that the whole series of Beatitudes is a development and an emergence and, further, that after the four initial clauses, which refer to changes in the self, we come to clauses which refer to that renewed self's activities on others. Now, as we turn from clause five to clause six, the activity and power of the trained self is increased. Mercy is an activity between oneself and someone who is in one's debt and in one's power. Further, in that sixth Beatitude we are still concerned mainly, not with what we do but with what is done to us. Apart from being assured that the merciful assure for themselves deliverance, we are not told what are the consequences of our merciful act done to some fellow human being; how he was immediately grateful, became generous and was a credit to our kindly good sense. We are not told that, because when we begin being merciful that happy result is not to be depended upon. Even the debtor who was forgiven the enormous debt of a thousand talents showed no improvement but went off and persecuted his wretched debtor owing him a thousand pence. What is guaranteed is that forgiveness, whether or no it produces immediate results on its object, does produce them on the subject, the forgiver. In short, the fifth Beatitude, though by then we have reached the stage of action, still does not speak of active external results but of inner benefits. The disciple is still being trained, though now he is being trained by doing deeds. He is past mere Proficiency. He is in the ranks of the Perfect, of those perfect because united with God. But there are degrees even at that height, in that final division. In the sixth Beatitude we then rise even higher.

Here we are told both of the large-scale work the trained now are given and also of the results which that work has on those for whom it is performed. The perfected worker is now an instrument through which God can express his intentions for mankind. It becomes clear at this point that the Divine Will is not to be content to salvage a remnant, but, rather, out of those who are first drawn toward the heavenly happiness, to create a type which may redeem mankind. With that clear, we can also note that the task is neither simple nor easy. All the preliminary steps are necessary; none can be omitted if we are to be in the end adequate to this tremendous work. For the task is to bring Peace. We are so used to a sentimental attitude toward religion, to regarding Christ and his Gospel as a mixture of lofty poetry and nursery fable that when we use his great title—Prince of Peace—we mean in fact nothing. Our mind's eye is filled with the romantic dazzle of Christmas-tree angels, of shepherds being caroled at by cherubs and fancy-dress magician-astrologers offering magnificent bric-a-brac to a shining baby. Peace, however, is a practical word and like all working words, it has its converse, it has its object. Like all real virtues it is a positive power directed against a definite evil. Peace means the force, the right force, to banish war.

This Beatitude, viewing the world and mankind, points out the first and most urgent creative act required of the perfectly trained. They must be peacemakers. Nothing else can be done till that is done. Healing, feeding, educating all must wait. Unless the perfect can make peace, not only in their own hearts, with God, but for mankind and between men, then though they themselves may be, will be and indeed are, saved, they cannot save the rest. The perfectly trained find, when they turn back to save the rest, that the peoples are not waiting to be saved, looking for instruction, inspiration, salvation. The peoples are absorbed, they have no attention for Good News: they are locked in an wholly engrossing effort, the effort to exterminate each other.

Two things then are clear: Firstly, that peacemaking is the *sine qua non* of any other re-creative act. You must put out the fire before you can start tidying the house or even examining the drains. Secondly, outstanding power, or, as we say, a miracle, will be required if that is to be done. As long as the house is not ablaze, quiet, persistent effort may get the kitchen cleaned, the windows mended, etc. But in the peril and panic of fire the wisest advice either only exasperates or is simply not heard.

How then, are those of the sixth Beatitude, those who are said to be equipped to help the world, those who are specifically directed to do this thing, peacemaking, how are they to make it?

To learn about that we must turn to the second half of the Beatitude, to the reason why the peacemakers are happy. They certainly would not be called happy if they had failed at the task set them, or only deluded themselves that they had achieved it, or simply returned saying, "We did our best, but they would not listen." Christ certainly was not a cynic. He took care to tell us that our Father plays no tricks upon his children—that He is incapable of deceiving them with false promises or letting them be deluded when they have trusted Him. He calls the peacemakers happy because they succeed and, further, he tells us how and why they succeed. The first thing that we notice is precisely their first title—what we may call (as this beatitude makes the distinction) what God calls them; in comparison with what the world calls them, their second title and description, which we must consider next. They are the peacemakers. They do not make protests; they do not object to other people's plans for making peace and preserving order. They make peace. The proof of the pudding is in the eating. No one will be fed if you simply point out that the puddings being made are poisonous. People must eat something. You must make one that people can feed on. No one will try peace so long as pacifism is simply a veto, a veto which, when the crisis has burst, quietly, courageously but unhelpfully tells the executive that all the plans made to meet that crisis are mistaken and must be scrapped. No man is free at the moment of action. The executive cannot listen, the machine cannot be put into reverse, the avalanche when once on the move, must run its course. How then do the peacemakers act?

That brings us to their second title. It is most significant to us, who are always waiting to see what our neighbors will think before we commit our own thought to expression. The peacemakers are called by men the Children of God. That certainly is miraculous. We might have expected to find them called impractical obstructionists, windy idealists, dangerous or harmless visionaries—but Children of God, recognized as such, not by Him but by man— that gives us pause. There must be some real, strange power here if that really happens. Indeed there is. And when we have gone through the Beatitudes we see that the power has not been lightly assumed. It has been patiently acquired. The charge has been gradually accumulated. Even those of us who are interested in religion still find it very hard to take it quite seriously. It is so thickly surrounded by words, eloquent or muddled, by rites, beautiful or conventional, by speculations which the more they are lofty the harder it is to see the precise difference they make to our immediate way of living. Do we really believe in a spiritual world as much even as we believe in a cinema story? Do we really feel that we live in God's knowledge, in His judgment, in His power, as much as we are aware, constantly and none too easily aware, of our neighbors' opinion about us?

Frankly we cannot begin to be peacemakers, and not merely critics of conflict until at least we know of spiritual power's reality at least as well and as surely as we know of the reality of physical and material and social powers. Further, we cannot begin to know of spiritual power, as anything more than a word, until we have begun to practice it. Thirdly, we can in this vital matter, only know as much as we can do. There were times in the past when the experience of others could work for those who did not experience directly. A living tradition was around them, a powerful authority upheld them. That is not so today. Each man must find Reality for himself. Quite apart from there being no "open vision" none who are acknowledged seers, there is no longer any living code declaring that the history of mankind has found that Righteousness is the rule of the Universe and violence the delusion of the doomed. Peacemaking therefore cannot be extemporized during a crisis. Nor is it merely a friendly way of life, though that is more than most of us can produce. It is, as the Beatitudes show, a tremendous culmination. Peacemaking, according to Christ, alone becomes possible when there has been achieved union with God Himself, with Reality itself, with the source of all power and the foundation behind all appearance.

That daunts many people. What then can be done? Views of what can be done and should be done—of the universe's agenda, depend on what we believe the universe to be. One of the chief troubles which arises from our not taking God seriously is that we are often in the ridiculously dangerous position of wanting to use Him as a means—usually when all else fails—but not to have Him as the End. That is impossible, that is phantasy: and in comparison with that the children of this world are wiser for a time than we. They must get their way and use their method when ours is such obvious nonsense. If this world, as we creatures adhering to it see it, is Reality, then its children are right: there are only physical means of getting your way, of reaching your end, for your end is only physical. However fine, it is only a material fineness and is attained by material method.[1] As we have seen, no man who can command a war machine would use it if he had anything more efficient. He uses violence not for violence's sake but because violent physical force has until lately seemed, to all save saints, the only way of getting one's way, just as much whether that way aims at physical good or at the bad. But if the world is—not unreal—but grotesquely limited and misrepresented by us, by the way our passions make us see it, there is another end and means save physical dominance and satisfaction.

About that other end we can be quite definite. The world exists for man to achieve union with God. The universe and life are the means whereby souls achieve Enlightenment and Liberation.[2] Cer-

[1] Cf., "If my kingdom were of this world then would my servants fight." John 18:36.

[2] Dr. Gustav Stromberg in his *Soul of the Universe*, p. 217, states as a final proposition, "The surface of the planet earth seems to be a place for the breeding and incarnation of souls."

tainly a physical Utopia seems increasingly unlikely by any other means. But a physical Utopia is not the aim. The aim is not a creature stabilized, bogged in physical comfort, arrested and even may be, degenerated, even physically, by mechanical aids to ease. If we prefer evolutionary language to theological, we can say the objective is the further development of consciousness until a new type of consciousness sees a world, a universe, a Reality which at present is concealed from our narrow apprehension. To return to theological language, it can be said that as the creative act of free will, of man rising above himself to a new union and a new vision, as that is the end and aim of life and of the universe, the first thing to be done is by so living, so enlarging, so being enlightened, to demonstrate to all men that such an objective exists, such a method works. Much of the present passionate destructiveness is due to men refusing to be satisfied with individualism and physical comfort as the ends of life and the meaning of evolution.

That then is the first step of the peacemakers, the re-creators of Peace. They gain the acknowledgment from their fellows that they have something which these others want. If they were offering criticism or good advice they would meet no demand: quite the reverse. But they are offering something which both they and others value. It is true it is not something which will instantaneously heal the world but it is equally true that few people want the world healed, really want it, as they want to be healed themselves. The peacemaker begins, like charity, at home. He must begin building up and out from that base for two integral reasons. We have seen the first: that men are first and foremost only actively concerned with themselves. They do not really want international peace, or even social and economic peace. But they do want, with a creative need, inner peace, peace of mind. Indeed they cannot really desire universal or any general peace until they have found peace in themselves. And here the peacemaker who is progressing meets them at their level, answering the needy according to their need. For the peacemaker himself is made perfect by making ever greater peace. He begins at the level of his powers and of his fellow's demands—individual peace, the solving of the inner personal conflict. As he shows others, by his life and power of peace giving, how to win this internal integration, they learn to look on him as someone who represents a higher order of being and who is an authentic guide to the dynamic way of peace. This is a first firm step. It leads to the next. He who has so advanced that others trust and follow and find, he himself wins to a new higher station. He has an authority and power now both to diagnose and to prescribe for group distresses and conflicts. Those whom he has healed severally will trust him when he advocates peace for collective conflicts.

For example, should a great psychiatrist be, as he should be, a great humanitarian, should he heal a great executive of some humiliating complaint (great executives are frequently, and not unnaturally, ailing men), should he heal him with a full understanding of why the patient is ill and what is entailed and required if permanent restoration to peace of mind and body is to follow, then the psychiatrist's duty to his patient, to his patient's work and to the social organism they both inhabit, is to urge the executive, for his own health as well as for the health of all, to use the same healing methods in his economic relationships and to show him how to do it. Hence we see an individual peacemaker, a healer of internal, personal conflict, rising naturally, by and through his success at the first stage, to work and success in the second. But, and this must be repeatedly stressed, he will not, cannot rise to this next stage, natural though it be, unless he understands his own nature, the natural-divine nature of man. He can have no power to restore the sick to the way of Life, unless he himself realizes that he must evolve and, even more than he wishes to heal his patient, he himself wishes to grow, to evolve to the full human-divine stature.

Finally when he has learnt to heal and shows that he can heal social troubles, economic frictions, he is ready for the third and decisive stage of peacemaking—he becomes the trusted ambassador of men, for each side knows, whatever may be its race, this man is one of them, this man cares nothing for personal prestige but only to heal. This would seem to be the way whereby the peacemakers ascend to even higher service. It is clear, too, that in these three steps of office we have the specific activities of those three stations of men who are dedicated to the service of God and man. The first station, of those who seek to heal the individual's interior conflict, is that, of the Servants of God. They are trusted by men in so far as their work warrants. Personally they are commended; they are confided in to heal private feuds. But no one thinks that thereby they could or should make peace between contending groups.

The best of the psychiatrists, the most powerful of personal counselors, has as yet never been thought of, in spite of all his successes, as the obvious man, to act as an industrial or social conciliator or arbitrator. Yet it is clear, did he fully know what he was doing, if he constantly realized what he already knows subconsciously, that illness which is now known often to be due to conflicts in the home must be due just as often to conflicts in the factory and business, then he cannot stop with cures which must be mere palliatives. He must heal the whole man, individual, familial, social and national. He, the psychiatrist, must not, cannot pause at the first step. For he cannot heal the mind-body complaints for good, until he himself is nothing less than a man of God with power "to absolve," with power on earth to forgive sin. Dr. Groddeck, the famous psychoanalyst, who used his gift largely to heal physical diseases, toward the end of his life was fond of saying, "How easy it is to say to the sick of the palsy 'Arise and walk' but useless (because there would only be a relapse) unless one could say the far harder word of power: 'Son, thy sins be forgiven thee.' "

So the second station is that of the Friends of God. They have more power, power adequate to heal social unrest. They can and have allayed severe tensions and guided gathering social energies, otherwise heading for violent conflict, into paths of productive development. Such a Friend, for example, was John Wesley. It has been acknowledged now by sociological historians that he by his prodigious effort in winning the love and gaining the leadership of the neglected masses, made British history an evolution and not a revolution, a process and not a violent interchange of action and reaction. But Wesley, with all his power and prestige, was able to do nothing to prevent the intense international conflicts which were ripening—the fracture of the British communities and the long destruction of the Napoleonic Wars leading to intensified nationalism. In fact, we see him functioning above the individual level but below the international. He turns economic and social issues into new and peaceful channels but he cannot affect the external fate of nations.

It may be asked was it not something inadequate in Wesley's theology and its praxis which limited his great gift? He taught a faith which believed in a God who would punish any who failed to accept His terms, with eternal torment, and which held also that by a sudden act of acceptance the soul was saved for good. Neither of these tenets, though they produce remarkable immediate results, lead to the highest spirituality and so those who limit themselves to such are debarred from the fullest spiritual powers. The doctrine of extensive eternal damnation, as religious historians have pointed out, made

[ 128 ]

many saintly contemporaries unable to support Wesley, a lack of support which prevented his teaching finding purchase among the educated: while the second doctrine, of full, instantaneous irrevocable salvation had equally unhappy results among his numerous converts. Wesley himself (see his controversy with the Zinzendorfian Moravians) certainly at one time intemperately and mistakenly claimed to have attained Perfection; a state incapable of sin. It was far more painfully obvious that for generations many Wesleyans claimed that they were free of sin while manifestly still committing it. They reached a sort of economic antinomianism— strict sexually but not at all strict in honesty. Hence the saying current once in Britain, "Never trust a Methodist too far in business because whatever happens he will wash away all his own sins on Sunday." Wesley lacked an adequate theology and psychology. He was of so fine a nature that he often acted far ahead of his teaching. He preached a God whose mercy was narrow and whose ultimate method toward those who failed to accept that mercy was an extremity of violence which the worst of humans cannot perpetrate. While so preaching, and himself being physically attacked, he practiced a dynamic nonviolence which repeatedly won him security, a hearing and converts. His theology, however, kept him from seeing that this, this dynamic love, was the Gospel and not the fear of hell fire; while his inadequate psychology kept him from being able to preach and inculcate such a training as he himself had acquired, a training which is an alternative for those who cannot experience sudden conversion and also is required by the converted themselves if they are to continue to grow in Grace.

In brief, he is a Friend, above a Servant and below a Son. In our own day perhaps we may see in Kagawa of Japan and Gandhi of India such Friends. It is clear that these men do much. But we can say more. We can see that their work is not only significant in itself, it points on further to a still greater need and a still higher type. Above the Friends are the children, the sons of God. And as the Servant can win by his individual peacemaking the acknowledgment from individuals that here is the way and on this way here is a guide; as the Friend can win by social peacemaking the acknowledgment from groups and social divisions and economic classes that here is the way and here is the guide, so with the Sons. The Servants allay personal conflict. The Friends improve circumstances. The Sons change history. Their role is to be healers of the nations. They have power because, through their innate spirit, men see that here is a type adequate to the task; here is one who cannot be doubted, who demonstrably knows all to be his brethren, fellow children of his Father. When it is said that men will call such a man a child of God this is no perfunctory expression, no courtesy title. It means that the common man will realize that in this man there lies the secret of creativeness and that through that power, and the acknowledgment of its authenticity and authority, through it alone will come peace. There lies our hope, but we must not delude ourselves. Though it is a guaranteed promise it lies very high, completely out of our reach as we are. We have failed at peacemaking up to the present simply because we have not had sufficient force. We cannot blame, we cannot censure the average man for continuing to put his trust in arms (yes, even in the present hypertrophied, inaccurate, ineffective arms) when we have given him little demonstration of spiritual force adequate to the issues with which he has become involved. True we have proved that violence used against lunatics is useless, unnecessary for our safety, fatal to the insane's cure. We have shown that the mentally deranged can be taken care of with athletic gentleness and often cured by a deliberate and deeply instructed kindness, that this is the most hopeful line of healing.[3]

True it has been established that savages can be contacted by a skilled and courageous courtesy: it has been established that social inflammations and fissures are able to be healed by those who come to the issue with a detached devotion to the welfare of both sides. Yet even at this level the results are falling far below those obtained when only individuals or small groups are being aided. When we come to international conflicts, conflicts now so

[3] The Quakers because of their nonviolent philosophy were in the eighteenth century the first, and for a long while the only administrators of mental homes to use kindness with the insane and they were the only practitioners to obtain cures.

intense that they can shatter all the foundations on which every other reconstruction, individual and social, must rest, we find no spiritual force adequate to the issue. Until that is generated and demonstrated, until men say: "There are the adequate peacemakers for they are demonstrably more than dedicated Servants, more than devoted Friends, they are actually, we recognize, the Children, the Sons of God"—until that is known and acknowledged we must expect war to continue. Men must have power to meet power, and if there is no true and actual spiritual power, power that works on the human will at least as well as violence works, then men will continue to use physical power. Fatal though it be, men will prefer to destroy themselves and their enemies, if this appears to be the only method of checking their enemies.

It is clear then that spiritual power has not been produced in amount adequate to our problem. We may add—it can be produced. We must add—its production will cost everything a man has, for everything he has must go if he is to be filled with God. If he is to become so filled and so transparent that all men own he is the peacemaker, he has power on earth to forgive sins, for he is the Child of God, God is in him. How that complete transmutation may take place is the theme of the final Beatitude. It was suggested above that these two final blessings come together, may be considered as parallel, because they are the two aspects of the one state—its aspect in Time and its aspect toward Eternity. The peacemaking Children of God are those purified of any wish but one—they have a single desire which has taken up their whole life and heart—to see God. Some notion of what this incomparable desire may be, the concluding reflection on the final Beatitude is an attempt to suggest.

# VIII.

## PERFECTION—iii

### The Understanding of All

✠✠✠✠✠✠✠✠✠✠✠✠✠✠✠✠✠✠✠✠✠✠✠✠✠✠✠✠✠✠✠✠✠✠✠✠✠✠✠✠✠✠

*"Blessed are the Single Hearted: For they shall see God."*

This is the final word for this is the ultimate happiness. Beyond this there is no progression. Here we arrive for good, for here Eternity meets us. Every blessing culminates in this comprehensive blessedness. In its light all the others are radiated and brought to perfection. Alas, we are used to such words—yes, we are acclimatized to far more telling phrases. We have heard, ever since we can remember, those eulogies of God, that polished praise of his presence, of the joy of Heaven. Indeed so hard has that kind of oratory been driven that now many preachers find their congregations more appreciative of a cautious restraint about Heaven and God. A sub-eloquent hint that perhaps after death there may be something, a ruminative "aside" that after all God may be in Himself a sort of Reality: Such ultra-cautious suggestions and feelers awake in modern listeners a keener suspicion about Eternity than the highest flights of rhetoric. How then can we speak of this climax of the Beatitudes?

He who first spoke them and they who first heard them, to them this was nothing less than a terrific denouement. That man should see God, should face the utter Reality, should look and not be consumed, should, indeed, be Blessed by the Sight, what a promise! As they listened, they listened first with puzzlement and curiosity to what seemed his paradoxes, where all the practical hard-worn values of life seemed turned over to show an unsuspected side; then with a growing poignancy as he spoke of the longing for righteousness, for a better world where men could live in a lovely generosity with each other, where mercy flowed in a constant circulation keeping far off the frost of suspicion, envy and revenge. Their hearts warmed; he drew them on to the hope that they might win that world; they might be God's instruments to change the present order of callous violence to one based on dynamic peace. They would have to be dedicated men to do it, but, as he spoke of it, how worth while it seemed, and, even more wonderful, how almost possible it seemed that it might happen, yes, even, that it might happen through themselves. The world, he told them, would call such the Children of God. A daring phrase, but it was obvious that no people short of God's sons could do such a thing— bring peace on earth—and had they not been told by their traditional teachers that they were the Chosen People? Then, with their hearts full of a new, strange hope, he suddenly clenched the whole speculation. To bring in the new order, complete dedication, complete singleness was the essential. But would that be enough? Yes, if that purity was attained, that would serve. Why? Because you would then see God! We can understand the sudden shock. We can realize historically the mounting glow in these simple men's minds as under his words the hard life, the accepted injustices, the weight of harsh government, the added burden of an inflexible ungenerous religion all ceased for the moment to be inevitable reality and another order shone before them, real, creative, eternal.

And we can realize historically the sudden change; the start, the glow eclipsed by that last daring phrase. No simple pious Jew but must have felt, "This is too much." No flesh shall see God and live. They were shaken to their depths. Was not this blasphemy? Yet the steps of his appeal had drawn them on as persuasively as a well-knit argument. He had been leading them along that "path of the right-wise which shineth more and more unto the Perfect Day." It all seemed clear and growing clearer, obviously right and more right until that climax. Many must have gone away saying, "We have heard strange things today"; must have pondered, checked over, wondered, doubted and then, with a sudden sense of revelation and everlasting relief, have seen that it was all true, that it all hung together—this was the meaning of everything, this was the Way, the Truth and the Life. True, we can reconstruct their reaction historically, but we cannot feel it, it is not ours. Quite the reverse. The heart, again, gives its inescapable verdict. We feel no thrill, far less any shock. Even if the phrase had not been worn smooth by pious familiarity, it would have for us only the amiable unreality of words. For God to us is a word: no doubt a great and good word but, like all words, something which has such use and sense as it still carries in virtue of the value others attach to it. Words are like money, they are of use provided someone else will accept them. They are useless if they cannot be exchanged. They are useless if we are in the desert alone. If everyone agrees that God exists only so far as they exist and have use for Him, then the thought of God by Himself when by oneself is apt to be the shadow of a shadow. We can gauge by the etymological thermometer how rapidly the temperature of such words, their emotional charge has dropped even in our lifetime. Even thirty years ago blasphemy was a word which had hanging round it a last vestige of meaning. Now it has practically none. No more shock is produced in an ordinary person today by someone cursing God than by a blasphemy at the expense of Anubis. Swearing is going out, for it no longer even sounds funny, still less daring.

If then we are to attach any meaning to this culminating Beatitude we must reverse the process which led to the first hearers' shocked enlightenment. They found it almost unbelievable because what was mentioned was a Reality which it seemed too good to believe could ever come into generous co-operative touch with their efforts. We find this Beatitude far less believable because what is still standing as its climax now seems far too vague and dim ever to serve as the fulcrum of action. As Godhead, God in Himself, the Creator, who is before, above and beyond his creation, is a Being very difficult for us to believe in, we cannot take Him as axiomatic as the Jew did. We must, if we are to be honest, approach Him as an Hypothesis. We must be honest, for we have seen the mess in which we have landed ourselves by well-sounding words to which we could or would attach no definite meaning. The Jew knew God was there and hoped, but hardly, that God might help him. "Our fathers trusted in Thee and Thou didst deliver them." That God delayed to deliver the petitioners did not make them doubt his Being, only his Will. We do not know that God is there but we do begin to see that power beyond our capacity, some immense power, perhaps infinite power, will be needed if we are ever to be delivered.

The six foregoing Beatitudes can in fact be used as an estimate indicating how much creative energy will be required if we are ever to cease to be unhappy. Happiness which we began by seeing was the demand of everyone, and indeed claimed by them as a right, has, as we have gone through this list, shown itself to lie ever deeper and to need still more gigantic force pumps to bring it up to our present arid living levels. Even when we are purged of self to the extent that we feel constant concern for others, are perfectly trained in serving them— can touch and not wound, operate and not infect— have only one appetite to know the way of Life— are steadily merciful in all our dealings—even then this splendid achievement is not enough. It will all be swept away as a foundationless structure unless

Peace can be established. To meet that final demand we have to draw on the vastest credit. Nothing short of being clearly the Children of God will persuade the Children of men, persuade them to give up using wrong force, physical violence, because they cannot believe in right force, spiritual power. We are driven then to call in the Eternal for nothing else will remedy the malady of Time. The disease is so grave that, we see, only some cure that is Divine will meet it. That is the negative proof—there must be a God or man is mad, a tale told by an idiot wherein all the wonderful physical powers which were to raise humanity above the floods of accident to a Humanist heaven, permit him to destroy himself. There is the positive proof also contained in the six first Beatitudes. The question must be met, when we have recounted these six perfections, what is it, what invisible attraction and inspiration, that has drawn some men, if not enough, to attain such superhuman capacities? The saints have always been appearing. To what power, to what invisible radiation are they responding? They do produce lives which within their range are superhuman.

Our proof at this point can then get us as far as this: on the one hand here is our practical situation; we have a clear estimate of the power needed to pull us back from the pit. It is obvious that the philosopher was more than right when he said about Happiness, that though it seems a natural wish, it is always only achieved by a paradox. You must never pursue it directly or, like Eurydice when Orpheus turned to snatch her out of the shadows, it must vanish. The hedonistic paradox is that only by aiming at something else, will you find that you have hit it. If then at any time the capture of happiness needs such skill (the skill of the fish spearer who aims at a spot where the fish does not seem to lie), how much more insight is needed if today we are to escape enveloping disaster? The only way to achieve an order in Time is not through concentrating on imposing a temporal physical Utopia. You will only have to go on liquidating increasing numbers of men because they are not fit, or will not fit into one's plans. We have to have a fulcrum outside Time ultimately if we are ever really to affect the things of Time—otherwise the revolutions simply revolve like a child trying to cross a creek in a barrel and the "more we change things the more they are the same." We must be transcendental if we are ever to be in fact practical.

Conversely we can see the effect on the lives of those who act on this estimate. Judging that only the Eternal can alter time, calculating that this great center must exist, they put themselves in line with it and expose themselves to its pull. They find that it does hold and sustain them above the deluge. We can then be like astronomers who, watching the path of suns that they can see, as for example in the Galaxy, discover the presence of an invisible super-sun, the shrouded but prodigious center round which wheels the whole of our galactic universe.

We have then established this at least. This final Beatitude not only could be true—there may be an ultimate Reality to be found, it may be the only rock on which happiness can find purchase, it may be that which has given the saints their unearthly joy and power—but also, unless it is true, we shall never be happy, we shall sink into disaster. This culminating blessing need not be dismissed as otherworldly—it is no more otherworldly than is a foundation. Neither, it is true, is apparent at first sight, but nothing would be there to be seen standing before one were there not this sustaining power beneath. We must then conclude by seeing what we can learn of this power and state. It is hard to say much for it almost all consists in doing, not talking. A scientist more speculative then experimental said to the great experimentalist Humphrey Davy, "I wonder if . . ." "Stop it," came the answer, "go and try." The conditions required for this seeing of Reality, this exposure to the mutating radiation, are simple. The instructions are contained in one term: Be pure in heart, be singlehearted. Then, as certainly as those emptied of the ego are in Heaven so the singlehearted see God.

But the task is the most difficult in the world. Take the first description of this state, "pure in heart." It is clear that this means a completed Purgation. "That," said the same voice as spoke the Beatitudes, "that which defiles a man is what comes out of him." You may watch your acts and words and even censor your thoughts but all the while a stream of infection seeps up from the deepest center, the seat of the emotions, the profound affective will. Until that is clean of its disease the whole man can never be pure. The second description of the necessary state gives us further insight as to how it can be won: "the singlehearted." We do not see Reality because of our fundamental duplicity. If the eye is single, we are told, then the body is full of light. This singleness is a fundamental lucidity, a power to accept, to see things without wresting them to what we want to see. Here again we recognize the ancient truth: the will, it is, which dictates what we see—and the converse of that truth: we must become what we see. We are bound to "impute ourselves"; we can only see in others those acts and motives which we recognize in ourselves. So, too, we can only see in our experience, in what befalls us, in what we attend to and watch, that which we expect—the working of a power like ourselves—like the force we believe to be ordering and directing ourselves. If I believe myself, wish to believe myself, a creature, irresponsible, not to be blamed —because of course I cannot behave creatively—the sport of chance, I shall see such a world, a world of chaos and blind Fate. Singleheartedness also goes deeper than a quiet and steady abstention from excuses. It not only has given up the wish to wrest things to its purposes: all its being has become coordinated round one transcendent desire. The singlehearted desire only to know Reality: at any cost to themselves to see God. This, it need hardly be repeated here again, is no vacant gazing or private rapture. It is the radiating of an arrested and sick organism with the creative light which transforms the creature into a creative being.

And what then? Should we close with an attempt to render in our vernacular those lovely but strange poetic paradoxes into which, in temporal words, poets and seers have tried to speak of the Eternal? They say it is that excess of Light which must appear as Dark: they tell that it is that terrific Instantaneity, that utter Presence, which is gone in the weary delay of a single word. We know the way to that experience, we know the need, the desperate need, the world has of seers who have so seen. We have good reason to go, and better reason to know that the Goal is assured by those who have already gone.

But, it will be asked, it must be asked, as we turn from gazing where the ladder of perfection ends and rests in inexpressible Light, "Now that the way is known and the goal is known, the goal which is the guarantee of life's meaning and man's destiny, now are we going to arrive? Now 'at this time will the Kingdom be restored to Israel,' will the poor demonstrably be in Heaven, the trained-meek inheriting the earth, the peacemakers, in the Divine powers as God's children establishing his rule here and now?" The answer is the old one, "It is not for us to know the times and seasons," because we do not yet know, grasp and understand the supreme mystery, Time. We have yet to see God. We see the way. We know, but have yet to see, the Goal.

The Kingdom may come here on earth. It may be a state, as the early enthusiast imagined, of "eating bread" in an economic paradise. But it may not. We have seen that in so far as we remain animals, physical comfort may prove as futile and dangerous to us as it proves to all other animals. If we try to put this issue in our everyday language, plain, bare, unpoetical, it comes to this. The issue has been confused both by the good poetry and the bad which has been generated round it, like steam thrown off by water falling on red-hot iron. But it is the most real and vital of issues and of questions: What *is* the Destiny of Man? The popular notion, which still hangs on—now more as a hopeless hope than as an inspiration—is that he will pad, insulate, protect and preserve himself better and better until, a perfectly arrested adolescent, he will gambol forever a permanent playboy. The alternative is that not merely his gadgets but himself should evolve. He cannot evolve further physically. Six arms would be an embarrassment, not an endowment to a creature who already uses of his two hands, one with increasing predominance. Six eyes would also distract a being who has already made his two come to a single focus of attention. Every muscle in the body has probably been modified and none added save that which works the tongue for speech. It is clear beyond question that man's specific evolution has not been physical but mental—the whole body has been made adaptable to a single drive, toward ever further-ranged understanding.

But mind itself has no finality. It is a hugh hyphen between body and something else, pure consciousness, spirit. That then seems his decreed destiny—to evolve and to evolve spiritually—into spirit.

The body, we realize, is a splendid, essential vehicle, but it must not become an end in itself. Every normal individual today realizes that whether he likes it or no, if he is to live into successful later age, he must regeneralize that basic energy which in the twenties found its maximum expression in physical power and skill. That energy will at this second stage have a less visible, more purely powerful expression and so mind will take the place of muscle. That many of us know, some of us act upon and there nearly all of us stop. We have to know that the intellect is far more powerful than the body. Man with his thews would never have taken the world from the carnivores. Indeed had man's spirit really cared for muscle we can see, from the gorilla, what would have become of his intelligence. Today, however, his intelligence is proving as fatal to man as muscle has proved to the gorilla. Our communities *are* mental gorillas, as strong, as stupid with their strength and, alas, even more destructive when roused and less able to control their rages.

That is why the advice of the saints is beginning now to sound like something more than transcendental poetry. After all, we have made such wicked nonsense of our powers, might not their vision turn out to be not merely beautiful but true? Mysticism, then, with its path of development (from the novice servants through the proficient friends to the perfect sons) would be no more than the continuation of evolution, evolution carried on now, as it can now only be carried on, through the mind and the spirit; and therefore also only to be con-

[145]

tinued by conscious effort, by man co-operating with Life, with the Eternal Life.

There must then be a third stage of growth, a stage beyond intellect as intellect is beyond muscle, a stage beyond mind as mind is beyond body. That our social distress indicates and the mystics' evolution confirms.

But all this talk of evolution, granted it is true, what precise bearing has it on our affairs, our crisis? We are not interested in the next Epoch, we cannot be. The next year looms so large and so menacingly. We were told in the last Beatitude that the Sons would be those manifest Children of God who would make peace. Are we, after all, only going to see, at best, the first emergence of a new species, a species which it may be granted may have the future but will certainly have to hang on for ages until the atavistic types have exterminated themselves? What we need to know is, quite frankly, what immediate, decisive use are saints?

To answer that urgent question exactly we must first define our terms. Sainthood, as has been suggested above, is a Genus in which are included three great species or stages of evolution. We are generally only acquainted with the first, the most rudimentary. When Michael Faraday showed his first toy dynamo to a lively lady she at once challenged the toymaker with, "What use is it?" The inventor of the new giant power maker patiently questioned back, "What use is a new born baby?" His dynamos have grown. No one now asks whether they are useful. All saints are dynamos. But the majority are at toy level? We may allow that, but we must also add that when they come to full size, and indeed *because* they have come to full power, we may be unable to perceive the current they generate then. We may only know it by indirect effects, so indirect that we fail to associate these with the generator. None the less that current may be essential to life, to our lives, as essential as are the invisible radiations of the sun.

Out on the Mongolian frontiers where three struggling empires wrestle, a traveler lately found a small body of Christian monks serving the desperately harassed native population in their effort to keep body and soul together. The traveler was pleased but not surprised. He was more surprised than pleased to find a little farther on another small group of monks; for these were Contemplatives, given wholly to the task of striving to see God. He asked one of the active monks, "Surely this is hardly the place for Contemplatives?" "On the contrary," replied the active servant of the poor, "we never work save with a group of Contemplatives near us." The active ministrants were the portable batteries to bring faith and life to a tortured, exhausted people. The Contemplatives were the dynamos to recharge the batteries. Invisible work generally goes before the visible. It must always attend it. The lichen which feeds upon the naked rock has that power because of its double nature. It is a combined plant. One part, the fungus, can consume stone. But this is only possible because the other part can feed on air. The power to be nourished by the invisible allows the plant to break down rock. So it is with the saints. Some are double-natured in themselves. They, the Sons, have become a complete perfect being, eternal in the temporal, walking in Reality, seeing through Time. Others, like the air-consuming part of the lichen (these are the Friends) combine with "actives" (the Servants) giving these actives their power of action. Without that contact with the air of the Eternal no real effect can be made on the rock and sand of Time and those who strive to do so do but become, like the dyer's hand, "subdued by what they work in." The primary force is always spiritual force.

This is extremely difficult for us to grasp nowadays. As a result of our widely degenerated spiritual climate, saints are rare and those whom we have are partially grown, arrested and too often at "toy" level. They are lovely miniatures and models rather than masters or full-scale engines. Why? These are mysteries but it may be suggested that our standard of sainthood is low because we ordinary people do not demand anything higher—great art only flourishes when there is an appreciative and critical public opinion. This rudimentary quality of our contemporary holiness is also partly due to the "seedling saints" yielding themselves to our ignorant demand for immediate material services—even for such apparently "safe" services as physical healing. They try to give us our palliative wishes instead of the real bread and health of the life eternal. They hasten to start yielding before they have reached maturity, a procedure which can only give rudimentary fruit and arrests the plant's growth. We demand soul-stirring preachers mass-produced in their lower twenties. We hasten to exploit any small shoot of verbal conviction or moving language. We arrest the souls we so exploit. We know this is deadly if done to any child genius in the arts, why not then in the realm of the soul? In the great Carlsbad Caverns of New Mexico it has been found that the giant stalactites not only look impressive but can be made to emit wonderful notes if struck. Some of these stalactites are quite quick growers. People run to find a new one and make it ring. But now these seekers after new sounds are discouraged. It is reported that the discovery has been made that once you have caused a stalactite to ring it will grow no more. It is fixed forever in and at the note which you made it prematurely sound, when, if left, it could have grown in silence until the depth of its tone would have arrested the most careless attention.

A graver case of premature exploitation of rudimentary spiritual power is in spiritual healing. All saints who have risen from Servanthood to Friendship know this, for their station gives them spiritual discernment, the insight to diagnose the soul. As they know how many diseases, physical as well as mental, organic as well as functional, spring from a conflict in the soul, spring from its self-will being set against God's, they will not heal unless their diagnosis tells them that the soul is prepared to accept God's forgiveness and to come into healthful union with Him, as fully as the body accepts the divine vitality, of which the saint is the channel.

But there is a further spiritual knowledge to be won here before spiritual healing can be safely approved. How is the healing done? By pouring out the divine life into the body which has become cut off from it. Then the sick frame becomes well. "And if there are no further physical troubles that is pure gain, surely?" No, not at all necessarily. If just being physically fit were our highest range and purpose then yes. But if there is a further range of evolution ahead of us, a growth in consciousness, a new awareness of Reality, of God, then this use of spiritual power for physical gain may be a serious mistake.

In the first place it may easily arrest a growing soul who was in the labor pains of its second birth. True, a being (as has been suggested may be the history of some of the Sons) who had never deviated from the way of acceptance might never fall into this coma of ignorance out of which a crisis must deliver the soul. But the general-resistance vitality of most of us is so low, we have sunk already into spiritual lethargy so far, that we are nearly always badly infected before we know we are ill and must then be "worse before we are better." We have already missed many warnings and driven through many red lights before we suddenly find the way barred. Physical disease is being increasingly viewed as an end process of constant disregard of the way of life. The calls to take the upward turning come throughout life. Those who answer the first call to grow intentionally, to evolve consciously, the call which comes in early childhood, they may hope to mobilize the whole body, assimilate it, turn to spiritual fuel the entire organism, until the physique becomes only a slower rhythm of the psyche, instead of a scar tissue which must be shed with struggle. With all the rest of us the body and its habits have already settled down so that we can never hope really to fill them with the divine consciousness. Sooner or later, as they cannot be wholly assimilated, they must like a shell be cast.

But there is a second reason why spiritual healing without understanding spiritual evolution is dangerous. The power so spent, so squandered, has gone in just restoring a physical equilibrium which may have been upset by oncoming spiritual growth. That power had, however, a specific purpose. It was not for physical benefit but for spiritual gain. Nearly all healers work by the laying on of hands. So they produce a restoration of physical health. But the Christian church started, by that method, its spiritual career. Still bishops are supposed to work in their specific function by this same laying on of hands. So they were supposed to produce or awaken a new spiritual power in those they ordained to spiritual functions. The healer today works spiritual cures but works ignorantly because today the bishop goes through the same procedure for a right aim—though he may not know it—but with no power. In short the power used in spiritual healing is the power to produce spiritual growth, to precipitate in those prepared by seeking, purification and exercise, the spiritual emergence, the spiritual faculties which belong to the spiritual stage of our evolution. Which is better: To have streams of patients temporarily healed of various physical diseases or even have everyone made possessed of perfectly functioning bodies? Or to produce new types and ranges of spiritual power, saints of such authenticity that the most worldly sense their power, Friends and Sons, Children in such Union with their Father that He permits them to order events and to shape history?

We need then to repeat that spiritual power is the only real power and that we too often fail to get it, indeed we are today in desperate peril through the lack of it, just because we can, at best, only believe in its first forerunnings and by-products: social services, physical health, material improvements. The invisible is always more powerful than the visible because it is the source of the visible's existence. Our low, weak senses can only pick up power when it has been broken down. The Cosmic Radiation pouring into our atmosphere is so "hard" that it pierces clean through our bodies without our knowing that we are being riddled. Of the millions of atoms which compose our body, probably not more than a few hundred are disturbed. Our senses can, however, pick up the echo of the echo of that deluge. The Northern Lights, it seems, are a tertiary disturbance caused by the invisible torrent which swirls in at the Poles. The saints which we see and acknowledge nowadays are at best secondary saints, more probably tertiary. The primary and the higher secondary are out of our range of apprehension.

The great star Sirius is perhaps the most famous of all the stars. Since the beginning of the Egyptian calendar men have watched for its rising. Then a few generations ago astronomers became puzzled by detecting a small peculiarity in its motion. One, greatly daring, said that there must be, quite close to Sirius, another star of the same magnitude; for only a body of equal mass could make that giant sun sway as it does undoubtedly sway. The telescopes of the time searched in vain. Then when the modern telescopes were at hand the astronomer was proved right. The companion star was found, an object far more wonderful than Sirius itself. For Sirius is only a splendid example of what we already know—a blazing sun. The companion was a "white dwarf," and that object was then a completely new discovery, an utterly unsuspected, unbelievable form of matter, matter so massive that, though it is a gas, a cubic inch or two of it may weigh a ton. But that was not the end of the story. For the discovery of the white dwarfs has led to a further wonder, again as much beyond all rational expectation as had been the discovery of the first of these anomalies. That was the realization that in the scale of stars, beyond the white dwarfs there must be black dwarfs. The motion of some giant stars shows that they, like Sirius, must also have dwarf companions but that these must be heavier far than the white dwarfs. These dark bodies are the most astounding objects in the physical universe. For they are so prodigiously massive that beside them a white dwarf is a normal star. They are so massive that in their presence, in the field and spell of their attraction, what we take to be the most invariable, inevitable

[153]

events cannot take place. They are so massive that light itself cannot get away from their intense pull (so, though they may be light they must seem dark). And, final astonishment, they are so massive that in their presence the whole process of change is checked, even Time must change-down and go slower.

Surely here is a significantly illustrative comparison? The first-grade Saints, the highest servants are the obvious, bright, flashing stars; evident, emphatic harbingers. The second-grade, the Friends, are still visible, but more powerful than visible. The third, the Sons, who can alter the very nature of things and change what is otherwise inevitable, they are themselves, save at the rarest moments, invisible.

We can then ask, when the Sons arise, do they come just to heal us or to reform our circumstances or to make us happy as we are? Do they not come, is not the only possible reason for their coming, that we "might have life more abundantly," that they may lead us forward into a completely other and greater state of being. They come to lead us into another "frame of reference," physical as well as mental. If evolution has not stopped, if it is now proceeding psychologically, in consciousness instead of physically, bodily, if it is now proceeding with prodigious acceleration, then that and no other is our fate.

We turn therefore again, with this scale of change in our mind, to face that old but acute inquiry: "Wilt Thou at this time restore the Kingdom unto Israel?" That question is being asked as urgently

[154]

today as on that day shortly before the close of Christ's earthly ministry. We put it in the vernacular of our time, couch it in the phrase of our day, as the disciples expressed it in their terminology, in their Messianic language. But they and we mean the same thing. We may smile with a sense of superior sympathy at their small vision and childish perspective. Could they not get away from their narrow provincialism, stop dreaming of a national revival, discard the blind traditional hope of Jerusalem a great capital and Israel a world power? Could they never rise above their prejudices and understand, however dimly, the awful august destiny which awaited their teacher, whom they felt might now make a bid as a Levantine Kinglet, the millennia of world history which his ideas and actions would affect, the incomparably strange fate in store even for their small selves? It is wearisomely easy to be wise after the event. Sometimes however the past's lack of foresight helps the present to discount its current prejudices. If we too are in fact asking the same impatient question, may not the astounding reply that history gave to their query warn us? It may warn us to check again on our estimate of our future, of our apocalyptic dream and tell us to ask whether we, like they, are not imagining something grotesquely below what the Providence of God has actually prepared.

Nearly all of us, almost every one of us who is influential whether we be religious or purely humanistic have persisted in looking for an earthly kingdom, a physical Utopia. Further, we have looked

for it to come soon. Five-year plans have been as
sure favorites with us as an apocalyptic cataclysm
by the time-of-seven-passovers was the current fancy
of the disciples' society. Further still, we also believed we should have to break quite a number
of eggs to make the ultimate omelette and that
part of the prophecy we have certainly fulfilled.
Final disconcerting resemblance, we, like the disciples and their fellow Jews have been amazingly
vague as to the actual conditions of that New Order
which was just around the corner. "The State," says
the most popular of modern apocalypses, "will
wither away." That is Das Kapital's final flash of
prophecy, vaguer than the old recipe, "And they
shall feast forever on the body of slain Leviathan."
But it is evidently, even in its phrasing, much the
same kind of wishful thinking, much the same
propaganda lure and urge to violence—and as easily
disproved by events. And then? We today in the
year of grace 1941 are living in an epoch of "and
then." Whether we recognize it or no, we are living
in a postapocalyptic age. The cold fit which suc-
ceeds fever is already upon us. The current form of

> The earthly hope men set their hearts upon
> Has turned ashes or has prospered and anon
> Like snow upon the desert's dusty face
> Lighting a little hour and then is gone.

The latest of the apocalypses has been Communism. It succeeded to and demoded the apocalypse
of the Political Revolution; as that had succeeded
to and demoded the apocalypse of the Religious

Revolution (the Reformation). And now the hope in Salvation through Economics has gone the way of the two preceding dreams: the hope of Salvation through change of Church and Salvation through change of State. The faith that ecclesiastical or political reform would bring men to inner and abiding happiness was dismissed with contempt by the Communist believers. They were correct in their incredulity but their own faith has proved as vain— precisely as vain. Their panacea has now been tried, and it has been precisely as successful in its appeal and as disappointing in its results as were its predecessors. In most places its party has failed to win more than a minority of effectives to its side. In the few places where it has captured the government the nature of government has reasserted itself in spite of the party program and protestations. Where Communism has succeeded it has gone through that invariable succession of compromises which leave as an end process the ground dust of a native tyranny instead of the cold ash of anarchy suppressed by alien imposition. It is this, the demonstrable failure of hope, of the current apocalypse, that is the most serious thing about our present situation.

The situation is grave: probably as grave as any past crisis. But what is making it peculiarly disconcerting, what renders it so much more unnerving than past crises is that the young and active have no dream of the future with which to make bearable the distressful present. We can no longer say, as others in similar travail have said, and so felt strengthened to endure: "We are suffering the birth pangs of a new order: the glorious revolution is about to break." The Revolution has broken. The Revolution is bankrupt. There are no further revolutions in the bag. For the first time since the end of the Middle Ages, Western man is no longer looking forward. And yet he does not know of anywhere else to look. So he still murmurs about a "planned future" and all his unintegrated, disgeared research still fumbles, like the fingers of a man dying of frost, to assemble a system of world-controlling knowledge. State education, state medicine, state hygiene, eugenics, compulsory controlled currency, controlled production, controlled birth, controlled death, somehow—if there is enough compulsory control—must succeed in making the world safe for mankind, for a mankind which, if left free, mismanages everything. And who is to manage for mankind—man! Nothing is to be left free and so everyone is to be happy (all save the one Leader who is to be absolutely free and so one must presume diabolically unhappy). Such is the Beatitude we have written for ourselves. Surely the strangest; surely more bitter than that till now called the Devil's, "Blessed is he that expects nothing: for he shall not be disappointed!"

Certainly the dream of a physical Utopia has proved as delusory as that of the apocalyptist. Is the alternative despair? There is a third choice and it is one which, it would seem, is offered by the Beatitudes and revealed in this the last of them. Instead of an immense improvement of our conditions there could be a far more radical happiness, a radical change in ourselves. Human nature could change: it could take a new step in evolution. We all now realize that the world we see is only that which our nature can register. If we could really have our awareness altered, if we could see the world without feeling greed or fear but with love and understanding, a new world would dawn on our sight. It would be something more than a world made possible, peaceful, welcome, by courage, kindliness, restraint and generosity. That were much, but that is only a beginning. The radical difference between our vision of the world and that of an animal's is not merely that we are more interested in more things and less frightened by strange ones. The real difference is that (probably through the help of this wider interest) we have come actually to see another, wider world. For example most dogs and cats and indeed a vast majority of animals are colorblind, tone-deaf and with little sense of perspective. We have then, by virtue of interest, actually entered on a wider world—the basic quality of our consciousness has been enlarged, something deeper even than our character.

Is not this a possible goal far beyond any dream of present prosperity, health as we know it, or order and content among men, even at their best as they are today? Here, instead, is a hope and aim which can expand with our growth. Nor does it leave us without a contribution toward the solving of our greatest problem. Mechanist, humanist, and religious all agree on one thing. This our habitat must fail, sooner or later. Our species is certainly doomed as are our individual bodies. That is a familiar fact. But more lately we have discovered how very mysteriously difficult it is to make any real progress, even physical progress, even in material security and happiness. We never suspected how curiously interlocked are we with our environment until we tried to alter it largely. The repercussions of those efforts have change our opinion of our actual powers. We upset the "balance of nature" and find ourselves attacked by disease; loosing epidemics, yellow fever, malaria, sleeping sickness; sending the soil that feeds us rushing into "the barren sea," and rushing in such volume as to choke the fishes in the rivers. We irrigated, and the salts deposited on the watered soil poisoned it. The examples are so numerous and from so many fields of endeavor that we cannot doubt that almost any movement we make to snatch a benefit overturns on our heads a compensating disaster. We are no independent exploiter of a virgin world. We are one of the world's children and very ignorant of the restrictions imposed on all creatures who have sprung from the earth and must live on it and by it.

When however we look out through our transparent blanket of atmosphere we begin to realize more fully our insignificance. No one can fail to grasp that utter physical unimportance if he takes a single glance through a modern telescope. For there he will see adrift through the whole heaven the star dust of island universes unimaginably innumerable as they are unimaginably, alienly distant; many so distant that we can only be aware of them by the light they emitted centuries of millions of years before our species appeared on the earth; the light they are sending out, now, will only reach this earth when, it may well be, there is only the world's death mask of ice to mirror it.

Considering how our knowledge has grown we are proportionately weaker than our savage ancestors. For though their powers were less than ours, the universe they confronted appeared incomparably more manageable. No one can ever imagine now that as physical beings we shall ever matter, ever shape, control or in any way affect this prodigious scene on which, for a split second of its life, we appear, blink and vanish. This fact, we must repeat, is now a textbook commonplace. But, because we cannot really face it, we read but have no reaction. We rush back to our former activity fearing if we paused to reflect we should be paralyzed. "Wherefore hast Thou made all men for naught?"

Yet there is a standpoint which would permit us to face the fact, realize it in our hearts and our minds. This universe we see is certainly unmanageable by us. We shall never act any part however minor on a pyrotechnic stage where our own sun is only a momentary spark. But what if we were not intended to act? "But surely that is futility?" No, there is another alternative. Indeed it is a greater opportunity; but we overlooked it in our itch to be busy, to be of immediate consequence. The alternative to action is being. We can choose not to act but to be. "That is escapism," we cry. On the contrary escapism is to play at acting when we know any significant act is debarred us. "But still we must act. For even if the consequence, the practical result is futility there will remain the nobility of our action in itself, regardless of results." That answer is fine. The only trouble about it is that it involves us in considerably more nobility than we really intended. For see where we have been driven. We are now compelled, not by moralists or idealists but by the enormous overarching facts of the physical universe, by the most basic realism, to own that we can of ourselves do nothing—except this one purely spiritual thing. We can act so purely, with such a perfect grandness and beauty in our means that the fact that our actual deed alters the physical condition of the universe not one whit, leaves no material consequence, that stultifying fact is somehow transcended. In other words the real meaning of our act is that it is the registration of a new state of being. We act not to alter the physical universe. That is utterly vain. We act, we can only act if we are sane, only and wholly in order that by so acting, so striving, we ourselves may become a new, further being.

But in what does this acceptance, this unavoidable acceptance involve us? It is all too clear. If our acts are not to be a grotesque stultification of our reason then we are confined strictly to such acts, such means as are themselves able to be considered as noble, as worth while just in themselves. Modern science it is that has demonstrated that the deadly doctrine of the ends justifying the means is as absurd and ridiculous as it is evil. Any of the ends of the universe are utterly out of our reach. Man's power really to affect anything here is a complete illusion. This discovery is both grim and hopeful. It is grim if we will not face that truth. The fact that confronts us is plain but terrific. We are not here in order to make any physical difference: but we are here, we can choose to be here to achieve a new spiritual level—or if that seems the terminology of uplift—a new range and quality of consciousness. Nor does that mean that we are denied action. Being can often be achieved by action; indeed is never attained save by some sort of action outer or inner. But emphatically it does mean that we are denied all of those actions which men only dare justify because they say they produce real, i.e., material results.

In brief we may only act so as to produce higher being; moreover the act itself, and no hope of result, the act and it alone, by its moral beauty and unadulterated nobility, is what must register and crystallize the new higher stage of character and consciousness. If the act is in any way less than this—let alone it being evil—if it is a mixed good, by so much it frustrates the whole endeavor and makes of the future life of man a demonstrable and squalid futility. We must repeat—for the issue is so acute, the opportunity so immense, the consequences so inescapable—if we attempt action, action divorced from being, action only justified because then and then only will we master events, we of all creatures are, by the unchallenged findings of science, the most futile and blind. We are blinder than the lemmings who rush in hundreds of thousands in a migratory urge down into the sea until their

[ 163 ]

drowned bodies mantle the waves, still blindly striving to follow a land route now for millennia foundered under the tides.

But if we act on this knowledge then indeed we may act, and by each action aimed at achieving the most singlehearted purity and nobility in means, we shall achieve that steadily widening consciousness which is the only possible outlet of evolution. As a by-product we shall have a world saved from the fate which wrong action must now ensure—the swift destruction of the species by itself. For, as we saw in the preceding Beatitude so and so only, by such acts and such creative being, do the Friends of God rise through His instruction and grace to the station and adequate authority of Sons.

With what picture of the universe are we left? With one which faces and preserves all the physical facts and at the same time gives incomparable significance to every human life. Here indeed is a vision which makes all our Utopianism, even the noblest, look as small and cramped as Jewish apocalypse of an earthly Kingdom and a messiah handing out the spoils of victory to his lieutenants. And it is one which found its first statement not in the mouth of a Hebrew but of a Greek prophet. The great dawn thinker of Greece Heraclitus is reported to have said, "Here we are as in an egg." Our soul, our consciousness is in this life undergoing psychologically an experience analogous to that foetal life which we all went through in the nine months when we were an embryo in the womb. Then our bodies were living a purely preparatory life. We were acquiring faculties, senses and powers only to be used when we had emerged into another life, a life incomparably larger, stranger and more significant.

We can make the simile apter than Heraclitus knew. The physical creature begins its life, at the heart of the germ cell, when for some twenty minutes the chromosomes confront one another and pair. In that third of an hour the fate of the creature is settled, the cards are dealt. Thereafter, all the rest of its days, it will only be able to play the cards then issued. What if our spiritual growth, the development of our consciousness, reverses this procedure? What if this life of seventy years is, for the soul, to be equated with those twenty minutes when the physical faculties and features were dealt? What if this life is not yet for action, for play, but for acquiring the faculties of real being, for taking up the cards which will be played when a full hand has been assembled? Certainly the stage, the universe—or, to be precise, this our present human apprehension of the universe—does not permit action. But it does permit being, becoming, growth in consciousness, if that is what we long for, ask for and are determined not to jeopardize by mistaken delusory action. Certainly the saints showed that a new species, a new type of consciousness can be achieved by such skilled and understanding behavior. And certainly Christ himself seems in his great parable of the talents to have taught specifically that this life is not yet our stage of action but a place which, if we are wise, we will recognize as an immensely significant anteroom. It is a testing room, a table where we are watched as we pick up and order the cards with which, as soon as we are equipped, we shall be called out to stations where we may indeed play a part. Then we may find we have a role beside which our wildest dreams of power and creativeness are less than the fancies which a child of three has of international affairs.

Such an outlook is startlingly unfamiliar to our age. Even with its present disillusionment with its own faith, the faith in physical Progress, it is not prepared for such a drastic "transvaluation of values," such a Copernican revolution of the mind. But before we reject it we must again ask ourselves the question: Will any other picture of things permit us to go on living? Some such vision of Reality alone can save our sanity in face of the universe as we now must see it and save our morality in face of ourselves as we now realize we are. Only those who understand that this life, this experience, this level of consciousness is part of a larger range, can make sense of and give order to this temporary section. Such seers of Reality and they alone can both "accept the universe" and save mankind.

We must not look back for the Future. God has always prepared for man a fate beyond his dreams. The Sons who have appeared have told us that they were forerunners, first fruits. The kingdom is promised "on this earth," God's presence manifest to all and everyone. Will that make little difference save to banish injustice and war? No, it will mean, literally, paradise, the recovery with an intenser consciousness, of that Eternity which we lost when by

[ 166 ]

our egotism we become specifically "man, the transitional creature," time-haunted. That is the only goal which can satisfy man and it is in that direction that the Stair of the Saints, the ladder of the Beatitudes leads us. At the first step we have men of right conduct, men who are themselves uninflammable but who cannot put out the conflagration or prevent it spreading to others. In the second we have men of right character, men who can prevent the conflagration from spreading to still unkindled fuel. But at the third we have men of right consciousness, men who living in eternity, always contacting Reality, can quench the flame.

These men are the aim of evolution, the one answer to Life's riddle, the sole reply to the desperate appeal of present man. So and so only but so surely we may believe it is the divine purpose to remedy creation by salvation and out of tragedy to bring a new wonder of being—to save man and bring peace by those who, by seeing God, achieve the one eternal union and at-one-ment, for they unite man with God.

Here then we close. Each of us is ordered to "give a reason for the faith that is in him." Here is one brief sketch. It may stimulate others to make a design that could be accepted by all. Certainly we cannot leave the picture of "Things to Come" as we now have such charts and plans, faded, torn, palpably out of keeping with so much of what we actually now know. A vast and increasing number of devout and faithful people no longer believe in an Apocalyptic Parousia, a Second Coming in the literal terms used in the Gospels, by St. Paul and held by nearly all religious right down to our own times. A vaster and even more rapidly increasing number of forward-looking, energetic people no longer believe in the alternative faith—material progress.

What are we going to put in the place of these two faiths which between them rallied the loyalty of mankind and steeled former generations to restraint and sacrifice? If we do not put something which attempts to order our knowledge then something accidental, dishonest or blindly fanatical, we know, will form instead. If you will not set a bone it sets itself badly. We must have a provisional picture of the future to direct our aim and to act as a moral criterion of our means. That picture the evolution of consciousness alone seems now to supply.

Hence this attempt to give a reasoned statement for our common faith. But the faith itself springs and has always sprung from that "reason of the heart," that migratory instinct toward a goal toward which we can go but which while we travel we can never adequately define. It is that invisible attraction which launches us, holds us, guides and speeds us. It is that which makes us singlehearted and as we so become we know that the meaning of all, the one adequate reward for all, the purpose and the end of all is and can only be this one thing, the supreme blessedness, Seeing God.

*Appendix*

## ON THE USE OF THE WORD *PRAOS*

❖❖❖❖❖❖❖❖❖❖❖❖❖❖❖❖❖❖❖❖❖❖❖❖❖❖❖❖❖❖❖❖❖❖❖❖❖❖❖❖❖

In the attempt to analyze the meaning of this
key word in the third Beatitude it has been suggested in the main text that "meek"—the English
Authorised Translation's term—is no longer fully
adequate to give us a clear and working insight
into the phrase. It was therefore proposed that in
this phrase there is (and should be conveyed in a
full translation and comment) a sense of something
more dynamic and constructive than the word meek
describes. For this reason there were employed in
the fourth chapter the words "tamed"—rather than
tame—and "trained"—as the step which leads to
being tamed.

This comment authoritative verbal critics have
challenged. The case against so considering the
word *praos* is that though classical authors such as
Herodotus and Thucydides use the word for wild
animals which have been tamed and trained, the
Levantine Greek of the Gospels must refer to the
Aramaic word *Inwethān*. Now this word is that
used in the Aramaic rendering (Targum) of the
Book of Numbers 12:3 where Moses is described as
being more *praos* than all other men, and in the
passage in the Prophet Zechariah (9:9) where the

[ 169 ]

Messianic king is described as one who comes *praos* "and riding upon an ass."

There seems little doubt that *praos* stands for a word the meaning of which is opposed to "arrogant," "domineering," "overbearing," "aggressive," "bellicose." But can we get nearer than that to its precise and practical sense? If we fall back on "meek" as being an adequate and full rendering of the word we are confronted, at once, with a textual difficulty, an absurdity of description which has startled even children. For, as we have seen, the first *locus classicus* of this word *praos* is in the summing up of the character of Moses, given in the Book of Numbers. Here the refounder, deliverer and lawgiver of the Chosen People is to be estimated in a phrase and that phrase is *praos*. It is translated as meek and, so put, it awakes such a sense of incongruity even in a child's mind, as to leave a conviction that something must be wrong with the text. The man so conclusively characterized, has had his history told. It is a saga which rouses any boy's imagination. Brought up in princely comfort, nevertheless his blood leaps, in recoil from his adopted culture, in defiance of his personal safety, to the rescue of one of his race; and not only to rescue but to hotheaded revenge of the injured. In passion he kills the Egyptian maltreating the Hebrew. He flees, but only to return: to threaten Pharaoh himself: to call down the ten plagues which decimate the Egyptians: to rally his people to spoil and then abandon their unnerved oppressors: to call in the sea itself to drown Pharaoh and his pursuing army. Nor is he more meek with the very people whom he has so ruthlessly rescued. When his leadership is questioned by Korah, Dathan and Abiram he causes the earth to swallow up these rivals and they "go down quick into the Pit." When the whole nation murmurs he has them smitten with diseases as though they were themselves Egyptians. When he returns from the Mount, bearing with him the Tables of the Law and finds the people, under the leadership of his brother Aaron whom he had appointed as Chief Priest, worshiping deity under the Egyptian form of the divine mother, the cow Hathor, he not only flings down the Tables of the Law in such rage that he shatters them to pieces but, his passion continuing, he breaks the image to pieces, has it ground to powder and makes the people drink a potion made of the sediment. When too old to fight he has his hands held up so as to rain down defeat on the native people whom his marauding tribe is attacking. He closes his passionate career by disobeying even his God, so violent is his resentment against the people whom he has led, when he strikes the water-bearing rock to which he was commanded to speak.

To search for one word with which to summarize such a character, to pick a single "invariable epithet" whereby to distinguish this man's difference from and pre-eminence over all other men, and then to say that that word is "meek" is to make nonsense of the whole narrative. Either the author or authors chose a word which summarized this man and then *praos* cannot mean only meek, or, if that is the only permissible rendering then the whole of the life must refer to some other person. The author (or authors) the editor (or editors) is a

[171]

skilled teller of tales. He has built up a perfectly consistent character—a man who lives before us as we read, a person whom we cannot but admire and sympathize with and understand. And because the drawing is so clear and distinctive, there has never been a doubt, down the ages as to Moses' dominant characteristic. He is the mighty passionate Lawgiver and Leader. In his hands are the commandments of Life and Death. From his terrible forehead spring the horned rays of Power.

No: at the start, with the first reference to *praos*, we are debarred by the mighty figure who bears this strange epithet, from accepting that term, as fully (or indeed in this case at all adequately) translated as meek.

Coming to the next *locus classicus*, the reference from the description of the Messianic king in the Book of the Prophet Zechariah (9:9) he, too, is described as *praos*. He is to come "*Praos* and riding upon an ass." Christ's triumphal entry into Jerusalem riding upon an ass a few days before his arrest and crucifixion, has made the reading "meek" ("as a lamb led to the slaughter," Isa. 53) seem adequate. But riding upon an ass did not, in the Old Testament, mean a lowly or unauthoritative station. On the contrary, the ass is a noble mount. In The Song of Deborah, after the destruction at the battle of the Brook Kishon of the Midianite forces of Jabin under Sisera, the Song apostrophizes the judges of the people and signals them out as "Ye who ride upon asses." Archaeology has shown that for a long while the horse was unknown in the Levant, even in Mesopotamia was referred to as "The Ass of the East" and after its introduction is mainly a creature of aggression—the war horse. (See Rabshakeh's taunt to Hezekiah when Jerusalem is invested and also the Centaur myth in Greece.) The ass was the ruler's natural steed. In itself it was no mean donkey on which you would hoist a figure of fun, a "guy" to be mocked. It was a spirited beast, in size approximating to a mule's height and of a speed which could outstrip a horse at full gallop. The Sassanian kings' favorite hunting was this speedy, mettlesome creature. Today Roy Chapman Andrews has been able to check up on their estimate of its pace and stamina. In his Mongolian expedition he chased herds of these equidae over the level plains and found by the speedometer of his car that they could attain a pace of fifty miles an hour and over before breaking from their full career. No horse can outstrip them.

The king therefore, who comes riding upon such a royal beast need not be any more meek and helpless than Moses himself.

But if the passive victim is an inaccurate description of the man characterized as *praos*, what word are we to put instead of an unqualified "meek"? If *praos* is polar to the arrogant and bellicose, is there no alternative to such attitudes but one of abject surrender? Is there not an alternative initiative to the initiative of attack? To turn back to Moses: True, he is not meek, hardly an Old Testament hero is less so, but reflection on his story shows also that the traditional summary of him as the inflexible Lawgiver is only an aspect, an extraction, a stylization into a single feature and conclusion of a character which the actual narrative renders far more successively and richly. The story is a liberal biography and as in such delineations of a life, we see, not a single fully-formed, undeviating will, imposing throughout its uniform impress on Egyptian and Hebrew alike. We see the development of a personality; the evolution of a temperament. And another thing becomes clear—as clear as the fact that here is described a growing spirit. We see that the possibility of this growth depended on a certain resiliency and suppleness, a capacity to recover a pristine freshness, enterprise, initiative, after every discouragement and failure. It is this inexhaustible power of recovery, this prompt dependence on an indwelling and upflowing divine life, that is the leitmotive which the author sustains throughout his biography of the Lawgiver. This is not inertness or flaccidity, any more than it is arrogance or self-assurance. It is a wonderful, inherent teachability.

Indeed it would seem to be most fully defined and expressed in an East Asian Scripture the *Tao Tê Ching*. There, throughout, what is sung and glorified in contradistinction from violence and aggressive power is this same unconquerable vitality. Therein "Lao-tzu" praises as the supreme force, as the virtue and gift which is most in accord with "Tao," this flexibility, suppleness, this ductile liveliness. On the one hand, he says, there are the hard, the rigid, the inflexible, the "ungiving," and these states, he shows, are states of arrest, paralysis, rigor and death. On the other hand there is Life and the Life-giving Power. It is most manifest by the soft-growing but always exploratory shoot, which will swell gently till it bursts the hard masonry that could not yield and upheave the massive inert

[174]

pavement. It is also shown by the yielding but irresistible percolation and dissolving power of water. And as with Moses, so too with the Messianic king. He is not a powerless protester and helpless victim any more than he is a victorious tyrant. He is the king who rules by divine wisdom. There is this other alternative to arrogance and violence. It is that alternative to war other than pax, the only alternative known to the Roman military mind, pax the armistice between two wars. That alternative to violence is in Greek Eirene—the dynamic peace in which alone takes place all creativeness, all enduring change, all extension of justice. The Messianic king can then be a true King of Consent, the sanction of whose rule lies in his inherent righteousness. There is another alternative to the contumeliously dismissed unsuccessful claimant. There is the king "after the order of Melchizedek" the Prince of "Salem which is Peace," the "King of the Age of Saturn." The epithet which is used for such kings is "mild": not inert, nor an underling but a benign overseer: "Mild and genial" as are designated those growing ages of the world when the glacial arrest is banished, not by fighting ice with ice, but by the genial warmth which thaws the earth, and the rigid and oppressive ice fields themselves into brooks and pools of fertilizing water. He, then, who enters borne by the mount of peace is not the mocked victim but the acknowledged spiritual authority who rules not by the sword of war but by the scepter of righteousness and dynamic love.

The character of Moses, the role of the Messianic king both require that *praos* must be rendered by a term more dynamic than meekness and passivity.

The king is one who has attained to this unquestioned authority. Moses' is a life which shows the way in which a passionate man was trained to acquire this skilled, unobtrusive strength. For the story closes with the great leader accepting the loss of leadership, accepting the denial of his lifelong personal hope—the entry into the Promised Land, accepting the fate that he must go apart from his nation to die alone deprived of the companionship of his followers and denied the attainment of his goal. So Christ's saying that we should take up his yoke is an indication of that training, that technique of being tamed. The illustration is, like all his illustrations, close-fitting to his subject. Character is to be trained, wildness is to be "broken-in." How? By companioned example. When a wild elephant is to be trained and tamed the only way to do so is to yoke it with a trained elephant. By contact, the wild one gradually realizes that it can become trained, that it is being set to a life not a blind thwarting of every natural impulse, but to purposive activity and a causal relationship. The contagious constant and immediate example of its close fellow bearer of the yoke teaches and trains it as nothing else can. It does not seem, then to be any straining of Christ's words, but, on the contrary, to be their close application, if we render his instructions about the training he was advocating, as rendering men who would undergo it "trained and no longer rebellious at heart." We are not departing from the sense and terms of his message if we indicate his instructions in the third Beatitude by showing that this "work of meeking," as a great mystic has called it, this reacquisition of

[ 176 ]

teachability, this attainment of dynamic mildness, is a long and skilled training. Certainly St. Paul thought of the whole of Christ's life as in itself a constantly acquired and extended training. He speaks of his Master as having become a servant in order to learn obedience, and of that training in obedience going on until the cross was its final achievement.

CPSIA information can be obtained
at www.ICGtesting.com
Printed in the USA
FSHW010507131119
64048FS